Life Is Like That

Reflecting on Stories
From Your Life Journey

Life Is Like That

Reflecting on Stories From Your Life Journey

Robert Codina

Whispering Press

McAllen, Texas

©2022 by Robert Codina

Printed in the United States of America

All rights reserved. No part of this publication may be reproduced, distributed or transmitted in any form or by any means, including photocopying, recording, or other electronic or mechanical methods, without the prior written permission of the publisher, except in the case of brief quotations embodied in critical reviews and certain other noncommercial uses permitted by copyright law.

For permission requests, write to the author at the address below.

Robert Codina/Whispering Press

robert@whisperingpress.com

codinaro@sbcglobal.net

www.whisperingpress.com

Book Layout ©2017 BookDesignTemplates.com

Cover Design by Lance Buckley

Photography by author and family archives.

Additional photos by dreamstime.com, various photographers

Life Is Like That: Reflecting On Stories From Your Life Journey Robert Codina. —1st ed.

First Printing, July, 2022

ISBN 978-0-9778182-1-1

Library of Congress Control Number: 2022906900

Whispering Press is proprietary to the author

Dedicated to

OMAR AND EDWARD CODINA

BROTHERS

Their life journeys on earth ended too soon.
Their stories continue

*"Like old photographs, memories begin to fade.
Events, people, places, life itself
dissolve into fragments from years gone by."*

Contents

Preface. Moments   11
Introduction. Stories and Tradition   13

Chapters.

1	Early Days	15
2	The Catholic Experience	17
3	The Freedom of Childhood	21
4	The Orchard	25
5	The Banana Rule	29
6	The Watermelon	31
7	Thanksgiving Turkey	33
8	The Chameleon	37
9	The Mosquitos	41
10	Death of One's Parents	43
11	Bout With Cancer	47
12	The Hot Streets	51
13	The Bread Controversy	53
14	Colonoscopy	55
15	Lost Tradition	59
16	Bad Hair Day	61
17	History Lost	65
18	Sharing	69
19	The Headstone	71
20	The Hunted	75
21	Heavy Issues	77
22	The Obituaries	81
23	Naming Your Child	85
24	Fear of Night	89
25	Altar Boy	91
26	Days of Old	95
27	Hot Summer Days	97
28	Embarrassments	101
29	Boring Days	103

30	Rainy Days	105
31	Surviving Life	109
32	The Church Experience	113
33	The Horned Toad	117
34	Apple Pie	121
35	The Mean Streak	125
36	Young Businessmen	127
37	God's Team	129
38	Monster Under the Bed	131
39	Dogs	133
40	Not To Be Outdone	137
41	Prejudice	139
42	The Fire	141
43	The Paperboy	143
44	Random Acts of Nothingness	147
45	The Mexican Side	149
46	The Beetle	153
47	Dark Memories	155
48	Portals to the Past	157
49	The Question of God	159
50	The Big Bang	161
51	Slaughter	165
52	The Old Days	169
53	The Pizza	171
54	Five Feet From Death	173
55	Halloween	175
56	Allowed To Be a Child	179
57	The Way We Are	181
58	The Cockroach	183
59	Smoking	187
60	The Violence We Bred	189
61	Marbles	193
62	Christmas Memories	197
63	The Meeting Place	201
64	The Evil Within Us	205
65	The Boy Scouts	207

66	Preparing Our Story	209
67	Reflection On Life	211
68	Epilogue	213
69	Author's Final Words	215

**"Life gives us moments,
and we give those moments life
through our stories."**

PREFACE

Moments

IN A MOMENT I was born. In a moment, I live life. In a moment, I will face death. Changes from moment-to-moment are not visible to the naked eye, almost immeasurable. The sequence of moments takes us from being a babbling infant to a graying elder. Minutes, hours, days, months, and years pass a moment at a time. Life is like that.

I do not remember my life in its entirety; I remember only parts. At any age, I can only recall isolated moments of those years. Our memories of life provide only fragments, but those fragments are important because they form our stories.

Some fragments are memorable, major events with great meaning. Many recall the day President Kennedy was assassinated or the attack on the Twin Towers in New York. On a personal level, people might remember their first day at school, a speeding ticket they received, their wedding day, or death of their parents.

Strangely, many insignificant fragments also remain with us. For example, I recall the lady who sold caramel corn at the corner store close to the school. I was in 4th grade. I can still see the large batches of sweetened popped corn the lady scooped and packaged in clear plastic bags. I remember the sweet smell seeping through the window. I would check for pocket change to see if I could afford a bag. Some days, I could only look through the windows, enjoy the aroma, and plan for tomorrow.

I can still envision the white-haired man with a mustache, dressed in white shirt and pants, and captain-like hat as he pushed his ice cream cart through the neighborhood, ringing a small bell attached to the handle bar. His face likely would have faded from my mind, but the image on the Lipton Tea package at the grocery story today always rekindles his memory and his treks through the neighborhood.

Memories remain entrenched in our brains. They are latent, seemingly forgotten, when suddenly images emerge from triggers in our present moment. We marvel when we remember events or details of life we had not thought about in years or decades. They have a life of their own, surfacing in our consciousness when least expected.

Memories remain personal and private, masked and shielded from others. Stories, however, serve as outlets for these memories. Through stories—a sampling of our experiences—we share a part of ourselves. We take these memories and risk sharing with others—risk because our stories can bring greater connection with those with whom we share or we can sow seeds of division and destruction which can destroy individuals and relationships.

Our memories will be buried with us in the grave, but stories survive beyond the cemetery. We are beckoned to share those memories through our stories before it is too late. Take a moment.

INTRODUCTION

Stories and Tradition

"ALBERT EINSTEIN WAS my great, great uncle; and that accounts for my genius." "I would have been queen if my family had not emigrated to the U.S."

People like stories, especially if they provoke sensationalism in their history. Family members do not brag about their father being a serial killer; but three generations later, descendants relish the details and share them openly with an air of braggadocio.

People find pride in being related to historical characters. They claim to be descendants within a distinguished or eminent blood line. Everyone who generates these stories—and few can be disproven—claim lineage from great stock. No one traces their ancestors to the town whore or to the village idiot. Embellishment and liberty are the privileges of the story teller, filtering and bleaching the facts to one's advantage.

Stories connect families, filling the gaps between the generations. The stories are shared by word of mouth and sometimes in writing. The importance is that they are shared.

Accuracy is not always the aim. Family historians have discovered the filter of the pen. Some stories are best forgotten and should go to the grave; or they should be sealed in a time capsule for at least a generation. However, these are the best stories; and they should not be lost.

At a primitive level, our stories report events of the past. They are experiences that describe what happened, when they happened, and who was involved. These stories are good for the history books. However, at a deeper level, stories capture the characters, the spirit of individuals, the relationships involved, and the importance of these events. Stories capture the forces that shaped history—our history—and describe those features that helped shape us into the people we are today.

The stories in this collection are based on true events; but the historical nature is not important. These are my stories which prompted reflections in my life, rousing a full spectrum of emotion and thought. They provoked moments of entertainment and humor; they stirred moments of sadness and remorse. Some resulted in life lessons; others concluded in nonsense.

My stories are not the focus. They hold no importance. The collection of stories are loosely connected as childhood and adult memories. They are in mixed order to avoid the appearance of a chronology; and each story can be read independently. They will prompt comments and discussion; but more importantly, they will trigger *your* stories for families and friends to appreciate and cherish.

This book opens the door for your stories. Others will marvel at your revelations, grimace in disbelief, share a chuckle, or shed a tear with you.

This is your book as you bring mystery and adventure, celebration and mourning, searching and discovery, beginnings and destinations. Life has much to offer; we have much to share. Life is like that.

CHAPTER 1

Early Days

THE DOCTOR HAD rough hands when he delivered me. The nurse had bad breath. Two others with masks watched from behind. The room was cold.

People seek to recall their first conscious memories of life. Some remember early events with extraordinary clarity; others are able to piece together only vague images. Most trace initial memories to around three years of age, but my experience was different.

I was anxious to be born. My quarters had become confined, cramping my restless spirit. I did not know where I was, but I knew I needed more space. Those initial contractions of my mother jolted me. I did not know what they meant, but as they became stronger, I sensed that those gentle nudges—now impatiently more frequent and with more force—meant that I had overstayed my welcome and it was time to move out.

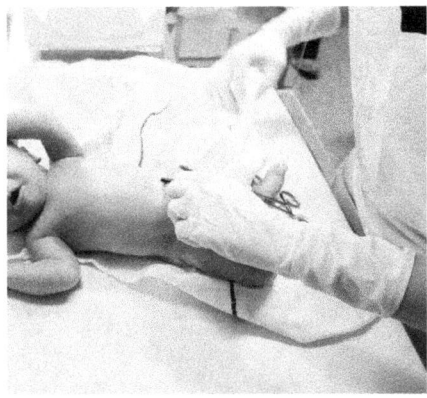

I finally could see the light at the end of the tunnel. I felt the cool sensation on my crown; and soon after, I caught a glimpse of first light. I could not make out anything yet as my eyes were adjusting to my new surroundings. I had no words at the time of my birth, but I knew I was beginning a new adventure in life. No one believes my version but it makes a good story.

I was born of Texas descent, of Mexican and Spanish heritage. My ancestry can be tracked several hundred years of known history, but my ancestry of unknown history trails for thousands of years. Any break in that trail would have made me someone else; or perhaps I would not be here, not even being a thought in someone's mind.

My ancestors of past centuries had no idea their existence would contribute to my existence today. Their trail of life resulted in my birth and gave me footsteps to continue their trail.

I was one of five children. I remain in awe how my parents raised five, especially being all boys. It was common in those days to have large families. I went to school with one who had 16 siblings; and I often projected how our family would have been similar if my mother had continued trying to have a little girl. Five boys were enough.

When we children were introduced, my parents assigned us numbers. I was son number four; and for nearly five years, I was also called the baby of the family. I never appreciated that term, regardless of any intended affection. I was grateful when my parents had their fifth child, and I gladly relinquished the title to my baby brother. I remained number four.

CHAPTER 2

The Catholic Experience

REGISTERED AT SCHOOL, I was given a name. I was no longer child number four. In the shadows of my brothers, I attended Catholic school. Religious sisters were abundant; and every grade had a sister assigned to class with the exception of the sixth grade. We had heard about this teacher when we were in the third grade; and we knew there was no way of avoiding her. She was strict and demanding, and she lived up to her reputation when we advanced to 6th. Given her character, she must have been a former nun. She lacked only the religious habit.

The sisters were conservative and traditional. They wore black and white, their robes covering them from head to toe. Their long black veils fell to the waistline. The forehead was covered in its entirety, preventing any glimpse of the hair. A stiff white breastplate similar to that of a stegosaurus lay in contrast to the black robes.

The garb shielded any suggestion of the feminine form, but an oversized rosary wrapped around them gave vague reference to a midline. This did not suggest their waistlines were evident —an image that may have given rise to erotic suggestion in those days of innocence.

We were innocent, living in a setting in which foul language was seldom heard. The "s-word" was used to call someone "stupid," and the 'f-word" was known to have a nasty connotation, although we had no idea what it meant. Of course, we had heard the "f-word," as we all had friends in public school. For Catholics, it was on the list of "bad language" which was material for confession.

Classrooms were not air-conditioned, and the temperature hovered around the century mark for several months. Even in full regalia, the sisters did not complain about the heat; and we never heard them under the worst conditions slip with an "f-word." They were disciplined, and they taught the students to offer up small inconveniences and sufferings to God. The sisters knew suffering; they had us.

Catholic folklore portrayed religious sisters as stern, tough, and demanding with a no-nonsense approach. Stories abounded how the sisters could spit flames from hell with just a look. Some said they could make General George Patton look like Mr. Rogers in comparison. My experience was different. The sisters were kind and gentle. However, I am sure they had another side to them which we children never saw.

I often wondered what happened behind closed doors when the sisters retreated into their mysterious convent. Rumors spoke of some who drank heavily, some who had mental health problems, and several who transferred to other schools. The last ones were lucky as they were able to escape the antics of Catholic school kids.

The sisters could have written volumes about their experiences in Catholic school. Sitting at their dinner table sipping church wine, they probably reconstructed the events of the day, each sister contributing to their collection of "tales from hell." From the children's perspectives, we were all saintly and obedient followers of their divine example. We were blinded to our own mischief and disruptive behaviors. We were young; and the sisters were tolerant.

Today, I would like to hear those stories from the dinner table. I would like to meet the persons behind the robes and shields. These were people who came from other parts of the country, who chose religious life, and who in obedience accepted their mission in the far ends of South Texas.

As children, we only saw the surface—the sisters as teachers who were doing God's work. There was a mystery about them, but I am sure there was much more to their lives. Now all are deceased or nearing the end of their journeys of life. As children in Catholic school, we proved to the sisters there was a hell. The sisters in their dedication and example, proved to the children there was a heaven. As an adult, I could appreciate and savor the stories from their dinner table.

**Photo: Courtesy of the Catholic Archives of Salt Lake City

CHAPTER 3

The Freedom of Childhood

AS AN ADULT, life is different now. We know too much. We are aware of too many things. Life suddenly seems more dangerous than when we were kids. This occurred when we became aware of all the possible dangers of our children's activities.

We perceive every person as a menace awaiting opportunity. We fear our children will be kidnapped or abused. We fear they will fall from a tree, be hit by a car, choke on a chicken nugget, or catch an incurable disease from a stranger. We restrict their activities. We keep them under our watch. We prevent them from venturing beyond our field of vision.

As children, we were adventurous, independent, and free-spirited. We spent the day riding our bikes around town. We fought off the dogs that snipped at our heels and chased us for a block. We crossed busy intersections, cycled down alleys, raced on the streets, sidetracked to events, and explored the unexpected surprises of the day. We organized neighborhood football games, calling friends who could "meet at the field" in an hour. We visited friends, walking a mile through town, choosing our own paths, even cutting through yards, climbing over fences, finding shortcuts through alleys, and running across streets. Our parents knew we were out, and they trusted us to be "good kids" as they had taught us. We were not wild or crazy in character. We were not hoodlums in the street. We were not members of a gang. We were expected to behave which we generally did, or as our memories choose to recall.

We kept our parents informed of our whereabouts, and they did not hover over us with constant scrutiny or smother us with parental restrictions. I recognize that not all towns are the same and not all neighborhoods are safe. Perhaps we were lucky; or perhaps our parents did not know better.

We were boys, brothers, and skilled in mischief which was a shade away from misbehavior. I am not sure if our parents recognized the difference. Mischief was engaging in a spontaneous rumble with one of the brothers. It was acting silly at the dinner table, making faces, and showing the other in a quick flash the food in our mouths. It was pulling a prank, a favorite being the placing a cup of water at the top of the door so it would fall on the brother entering the room.

The line into misbehavior was crossed when the mischief ended differently than expected—breaking the lamp while rumbling, knocking the dinner plate to the floor, or having the water spill on our father. We were often in tears while laughing at our mischief; we were often in tears because of our misbehavior. We could be disciplined, redirected, and punished with consequences; but on occasion, time was short and the belt spoke for itself. I forgot any words spoken to us but I remember the belt. Fortunately, a spanking was not frequent; and it was usually with the hand.

As I reflect on my early years, I recall many incidents which were insignificant at the time. Now I can appreciate the experiences, how they helped shape my childhood feelings about life.

Perhaps I am being delusional or selective in my memories; but overall, I characterize myself as having been a happy child. I never thought in those terms when I was growing up. I just lived life; and the consequence of events seemed to add up to that conclusion.

I attribute much to my parents. They were not aware of their contributions; but in their family structure of values and guidance to their five sons, they provided us the greatest gift of childhood—they allowed us to be children.

CHAPTER 4

The Orchard

I LIKE TO BELIEVE we lived in years of innocence. In retrospect, we lived in years of ignorance. We were oblivious to danger around us. I wonder today if our parents were aware of the dangers. Of course, those times were different. People trusted more; and boys could take care of themselves.

We lived at a time when people still hitchhiked. It was common to see people with thumbs outstretched in the air and a backpack on their shoulder. Offering a ride to a needy traveler was considered a good deed.

I could tell by looking at hitchers whether they were dangerous. "They just had that look." I credited myself as being gifted in judging people. Social scientists have never been able to isolate and define *that look*. Perhaps I was ahead of my time, but I eventually matured. I caught up with myself and confirmed how naive I really was.

On one occasion, while walking home from the public library, a car passed slowly. I had a strong suspicion it would venture back. The driver had *that look*. My instinct was confirmed and the car made a u-turn, slowed, and pulled to the curb. The young driver, perhaps 24, asked if I wanted a ride. In my mature 11-year-old judgment, I consented and entered the car alone with him.

He seemed friendly—aren't they always—and he asked if he could make a stop before dropping me off. What could I say?  I was not behind the wheel. He proceeded to the outskirts of town and pulled into an orchard. By this time, I figured he was not there for the oranges. I kept a watchful eye, my mind rehearsing possible scenarios that might unfold. My fight or flight instinct set in, but the mental debate stalemated and I did neither.

The two of us were in the front seat. With the car parked in a clearing among the trees, he cut the motor. He looked over at me, his eyes frisked my body, and he asked if I wanted to open my pants. I declined with an innocent "No, I'm okay" and to my surprise, he accepted my response without further pursuit. He excused himself and went into the orchard.

This was my chance to flee but in the moment, I waited instead. He had done nothing to me, and I wanted a ride back into town. He returned to the car and dropped me at a grocery store where I had told him I had planned to meet a friend. I did not want him to know where I lived in case he had an urge to visit the orchard again.

These are the kind of stories one sees in the news today. My experience could have ended tragically. I could have been one of those missing children whose decomposed body would not be found for days. My life could have ended at 11 years. I wonder at times whether the young man who approached me is still alive today and if he remembers the incident. I thank him for being respectful in his disrespectful overture. He could have been forceful, violent, and overpowering on my small stature. We learn through our experiences, if we are fortunate to live through them.

Our childhood experiences are potent. We can gain understanding of life and share wisdom with our children; or we can coil in fear and become overprotective. In the latter, we risk shaping our children with a warped reality and with an unhealthy outlook which we justify as a way of protecting them from danger. Parents struggle in finding the balance. Children struggle in not knowing the balance. Life is not intended to cage us, even under the guise of safety.

CHAPTER 5

The Banana Rule

THE FAMILY RULES were never posted in the house but they were known. We were five children—all boys—so I surmise the rules served as a parental lasso to maintain some semblance of family order. We were not angelic children, but we were obedient within the broader definition of being boys. We were also Catholic, so disobedience was not only accountable to our parents but also to God. "Honor your father and your mother" was one commandment we learned by heart. As a child, I always found it easier to face God.

Besides the rules, our parents had informal guidelines—those expectations parents instilled in their children. They served as quips of wisdom to guide us in life. We understood the basic ones like not running with scissors or with pencil in hand to avoid poking your eye out, or not talking with your mouth full during a meal. These made sense to us, although flashing my open mouth filled with food to one of the brothers always elicited a grossed out but funny response.

The banana rule was different. "Don't eat bananas at night," our mother would always tell us. Respectful, I did not question; obedient, I complied. Some things become ingrained in the mind, rooted in childhood and carried into adult years. "Wash your hands before you eat, brush your teeth before you go to bed, say please and thank you…and don't eat bananas at night."

As a young adult, I shuffled my cart through the fruit section of the supermarket. I experienced a flashback of the banana rule. My mother had died more than 15 years prior, but I could see her face, her voice unmistakable.

"Don't even think about it," her command echoed in my head; and my response returned to childhood feelings of obedience. I slowed in the aisle, peered at the stacks of vibrant yellow bananas beckoning me. I checked my watch; evening

was approaching. Night would soon be here. A knot in my stomach began to form, and temptation teased my conscience.

I caved to my cravings and selected the largest bunch. "Be careful. Wait until you get home," I thought, "in case something happens."

That night I let my guard down and betrayed my conscience. Darkness had already settled. I ripped the banana with great anticipation and anxiety. I hesitated, took a small nibble, and paused; and then I quickly devoured the rest. I froze in my chair, closed my eyes, and waited. "What is supposed to happen?" I experienced no sensations, no physical reaction. My mind was still clear. "Perhaps I needed to eat a second."

I never understood the advice given by my mother. For years, I had conceded obediently to her advice. Perhaps she had learned the banana rule from her mother; and perhaps she lived in unquestionable obedience. I slept well; but that night, I transitioned in a small way into adulthood.

CHAPTER 6

The Watermelon

BANANAS WERE NOT the only fruit with rules. Watermelons had their own set; but unlike bananas, we were free to eat watermelons at any time of the day or NIGHT.

Watermelons were grown locally, so they were plentiful and cheap. Roadside fruit stands were everywhere. Anyone with a pickup truck could park along the highway and sell their load of melons—no license, no health certificate, no knowledge whether they had been stolen from a neighboring field the night before. For 50 cents, we could choose the pick of the lot. Of course, we wanted the biggest one for the money; but we also wanted the sweetest and the juiciest.

We had our method for choosing. First, ensuring there were no bruises or cracks in the rind, we would look for the round melons because they had a dark red meat inside. Sometimes we had to settle for the long melons with a lighter, almost pinkish tone. To us, they really tasted the same, but the deep red color looked juicer and ready to eat. Then we would give it a thump or two as we pressed our ear to the rind. "Hmmm, let's try that other one to compare." We had no science to our method, but it made us feel and look intelligent—at least to friends who accompanied us and who were unfamiliar with the rule of thumping. They always seemed impressed. The vendor was not, but he said nothing as long as we made a purchase.

Watermelons, however, came with cautions. At least two rules had circulated among the neighborhood kids. We were told to be cautious about swallowing the seeds because they would find refuge in our appendix. We did not know where the appendix was exactly but it had to be close to the stomach. How a seed knew to go the appendix and not to the stomach was beyond our comprehension. We had not taken biology yet.

We loved watermelons on a hot summer day, and we did not care if an errant seed went down with the melon. Some melons had excessive seeds, and trying to spit them out while eating a slice was bothersome and inefficient. Swallowing a few seeds was inevitable. We had heard of a few kids who were hospitalized having their appendices removed; and we took this as a red flag, a cautious reminder that our appendix did not have an infinite capacity.

Not everyone was told about the appendix. One girl was cautioned about the seeds becoming implanted in the stomach where they could begin to grow inside the human body. Imagination can draw fear when one does not know better. We had seen young women with growing bellies, and our innocence did not understand. As we matured, we discovered the truth. It was the stork, not the watermelon seeds.

I do not know who established the fruit rules. As children, we were impressionable; and I wondered why other fruit did not have rules. What about mangoes, papayas, tangerines, or pomegranates? Had our parents been withholding information from us as children? Were they protecting us from dangers we did not see? In any case, several years later, we were introduced to the seedless watermelon. At last we felt safe.

CHAPTER 7

Thanksgiving Turkey

THANKSGIVING ALWAYS MEANT turkey, but something was different. The frozen bird always had to defrost for a few days in the refrigerator. It was not there and I peeked into the freezer. I only saw Popsicles and ice trays, but no turkey.

Within the hour, my father pulled up to the house in his old work truck. He was not with anyone, but he was not alone. He exited the vehicle with a live, fully feathered turkey, squawking nervously as any turkey would do around Thanksgiving. The turkey must have sensed his fate. We had never prepared a live gobbler, so we waited in anticipation how all this was supposed to work.

My father knew what he was doing. He entered the garage with clear intent and grabbed the long-handled axe. We only had known the axe for cutting firewood on camping trips and to pound stakes into the hard ground when setting up tents. The axe never served as a weapon, but we saw what was coming. We kept a safe distance as my father stabilized an old flat-topped log as the beheading table.

One quick swoop and I thought it would be finished. His head was off, and the turkey was supposed to fall over. He had different plans, as he ordained his last act of revenge. With his motionless head on the ground, his body darted from the butchering block. He took a few zig-zagging steps, turned, and aimed directly at my brother and me. He obviously did not see us, but he continued his frenzied trot in our direction—a turkey without a head chasing two small kids.

We made it to the back door of the house as the turkey plopped over and lay motionless. I did not trust it. I had seen too many horror movies, and I envisioned the lifeless bird making one final lunge toward us.

We did not wait to check it out, but we felt relatively assured he was dead once it was placed in the oven. We debated for the remainder of the afternoon how a headless turkey had managed to chase two terrified children. He could have fallen over and floundered on the ground until he died. He could have run aimlessly in any direction. He could have attacked the henchman who was responsible for his beheading. No, he targeted two panic-stricken children who took some consolation in running faster than the turkey.

We drew no conclusions; and the mystery remained unsolved. In the end, we welcomed the turkey to our Thanksgiving table.The experience was traumatizing for a while, but I did not let it affect me too long. It became the talk of the neighborhood for the next two months; and the family added the story to its oral tradition recited every year at the dinner table. I still eat turkey, and I continue the tradition of having it as the main course on Thanksgiving. I buy the turkey frozen or fresh.

I do not know if the experience affected my brother who was also chased. He eventually became a vegetarian, and I always wondered if there was some connection to this childhood event.

That was the only time my father brought home a live turkey; and I never inquired further about it. Perhaps a friend had bartered with my father, exchanging the turkey for some merchandise from his business. Perhaps, he wanted to ensure a fresh turkey at the table. Personally, I think he had an axe to grind; but after that experience, I decided it was time to bury the axe.

CHAPTER 8

The Chameleon

THE NEAREST ZOO was 250 miles away, so the local pet shop was the best option. There were no giraffes, gorillas, or antelopes; but on a smaller scale, we were thrilled in watching and touching the snakes, turtles, rabbits, white rats, and guinea pigs. Stocked aquariums lined the wall, filled with tetras, neons, zebra fish, black mollies, and guppies. As kids, we could afford to buy these.

The fancy fish were bright and colorful—the salt water variety—and of course they were more expensive and beyond our budget. Goldfish were colorful and inexpensive, but they were known to pollute the aquariums as they were always seen with long strings of dangling fecal matter like a small airplane flying an advertising banner. We learned to avoid goldfish except at carnivals and school fairs which always awarded them as prizes. We loved winning but we hated the goldfish.

The pet shop introduced a new species to its collection, the chameleon. How novel, we thought, to have a lizard as a pet. They were small, manageable for a child, and only 4-5 inches in length. They were shaded in green with a sagging red throat which flared out when excited or threatened. This was a pet to be shared, certainly fascinating, and a conversation piece. We did not hesitate.

It was the latest fad—well, one we decided to start—and what better place than at school to show off the next day. Three of us—all classmates in the 8th grade—paraded around with chameleons on our shoulders, attached to 6-inch leashes which were provided with the purchase.

Wrapped around his neck, the leash irritated the lizard. With no space to roam, the chameleon settled on my shoulder, propped on his hunched legs, and he swayed back and forth ready to jump. Turning my head toward him, he shifted his slithering body in my direction, locked his piercing eyes with

mine and lifted his rubbery brow. He was conniving.

"What is he up to?" I thought. I felt his restless spirit, and I conceded by giving him more freedom. I extended his short leash, attaching a longer string so he could wander freely about my body. He appeared more relaxed as he shifted his neck back and forth. He smacked his mouth two times which I interpreted as his way of saying "thank you."

At recess, I stepped into the courtyard at the same time the chameleon took a leap from my shoulder into the air in its stretch for freedom. The string was too long, and he vaulted to the ground as I paced forward. There was no avoidance as my foot and the weight of my body mashed its tender form against the unforgiving concrete. I reeled in the extended leash to scrutinize the damage. He was not injured or bruised. He was dead.

The fad ended the same day it started. After seeing the dead chameleon on the leash, no other classmates thought it stylish to own one. I knew the pet shop would not accept returns, so I discarded the limp body unceremoniously into the trash can. I felt no grief for we had not bonded in our short time together. I had not even given him a name.

I realized the chameleon was not created to be confined, constrained by a 6-inch leash, nor to be worn as some cheap costume jewelry; and I felt saddened that his new-found freedom had so quickly been trampled underfoot.

CHAPTER 9

The Mosquitoes

MOSQUITOES WERE BORN for intimacy with humans. Heavy rains, a humid environment, and deprived appetites offered the perfect storm for mosquitos to invade.

They can be absent one day; and after a heavy downpour, millions emerge in search of red meat. They have a strategy with people, and they orchestrate it to perfection. They attack in numbers—some cause distraction while others approach in stealth mode. They target with precision, able to bite the exact spot on the back where one's hands cannot reach. They penetrate the clothing and drill until they have their fill.

As kids, we marveled on swatting a mosquito and showing our kill to each other. "Wow, look how much blood this one had," we exclaimed without realizing it had been freshly drawn from our neck.

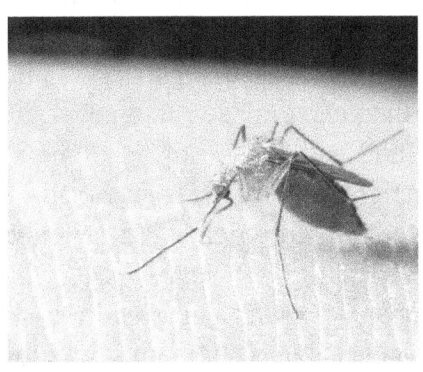

When the mosquitos converged in full force, the city waged war on them by spraying the neighborhoods. The fumigator resembled a large cannon attached to the city truck; and it rolled slowly through the streets expelling a large cloud of pesticide. We could hear the machine sputtering as it drew closer to the house while we jumped excitedly announcing it was coming.

We darted outside behind the fumigator and disappeared into the fog, laughing and yelling in our fantasies. What these fantasies were at the time have been lost in faded memories, probably directly related to the pesticide I ingested. The fumigator always signaled a special occasion. Playing in the fog was entertaining; and all the children in the neighborhood reveled in the experience. It became the talk at the school the next day.

Parents never warned breathing the vapors might be harmful. The city never publicized cautions before the spray; and they never stopped the children from running into the streets during the operations. The kids in the neighborhood joined in freely in the neighborhood event and they never complained of sickness or foul consequences.

The city still fumigates on occasion, although not as often as when we were kids. Over the years, my son was never able to experience the excitement and anticipation of the rumbling fumigator approaching the neighborhood. He never had the opportunity of getting lost in the fog with friends. He never had the chance to inhale the misty pesticide.

"One man's fun is another man's poison" and as children, we had the best of both. We survived, but some some traditions should be laid to rest.

CHAPTER 10

Death of One's Parents

"YOUR MOTHER IS DEAD." These are hard words to process at any age. What am I supposed to say, to think, to feel when the moment arrives?

As a child, I often wondered how I would react with news my parents had passed away. It is a child's way of trying to cope with the inevitable—someday, somehow, they will no longer be with us. Perhaps it is a primitive attempt to address the issue of death. As a child, death is abstract and a reality not well understood in the mind of one who has little to no experience in this matter. It lies ambiguously in the future—a time which may be imminent or at some distant point.

Parents do not always die first. I wondered if I might precede their passing. My parents did die, seventeen years apart, and my images of rehearsal for their deaths never came to mind. I was in my first year of college away from home when I received the telephone call at night my mother had been in a car accident and did not survive.

Like old photos, mental images of my mother have faded since her death decades ago. A few emotional strands remain in memory. Occasional experiences—a conversation with an old family friend or relative—will capture a moment or snapshot of days gone by. Her life of 46 years has been reduced to these fleeting morsels. At age 19, I reflected on how she had been able to live a relatively full life. Now that I have passed her age,

I realized how young she really was. Perspective changes with time.

My father died at 72. He was aware of his aortic aneurysm and knew that someday it might burst. A call at night complaining of "kidney pains" prompted a rush to the hospital. Someday had arrived. He had hours to live. The doctor suggested I inform him. I had no practice in doing this; it was not part of my rehearsal. My father's reaction upon being told he was on his deathbed was disappointment. "Before Thanksgiving?" It was two days prior to the holiday, and he had planned to smoke a turkey for family and friends.

He slipped slowly into unconsciousness within the next hour, surrounded by a few close friends. I was the only son who had arrived at the hospital on time. I had transported him, not knowing the severity of his condition. No rehearsal for his death would have sufficed. I cherished the moments of being by his side—helpless to do anything, but more importantly, just to be present. The lessons of old materialized: our days are numbered, ours breaths are counted. Finality had set in, and I witnessed the end of one's cycle of life.

My father had just died. No medical personnel were in the room and I wondered what was to follow. I informed staff at the nurse's station and was told that the funeral home would send a hearse "to pick up the remains." The corpse was not the essence of my father, so technically "the remains" was correct. The words of the moment, however, appeared insensitive and dehumanizing. A person, a man, a father, MY father, could be reduced to remains in a matter of minutes.

Both parents were now deceased. This realization echoed in my head. Emotionally, I was still numb. There is an unspoken assurance and feeling of security knowing at least one parent is still living. The connection was now severed, and it was the end of a generation.

Psychologists say it is important to bring closure to their passing. I prefer to use the term "to embrace their passing. Closure suggests "wrapping it up" or "acceptance so one can move on." Yes, a chapter of life did close, but their book of life remained open to me.

I have grown older. I have made many decisions, chosen life paths, and made life choices. I realized that my parents had faced the same questions, in their time and in their way. While I was growing up, they were "mom and dad" to me; and I did not comprehend beyond those labels.

Now I can appreciate them more fully because I have travelled the same road of life. I see them more clearly. I see their footsteps on my own life path; I sense their spirit on the road ahead of me. There is no closure, and I embrace them in their passing.

"In their younger days"

CHAPTER 11

Bout With Cancer

EVEN WITH FAMILIES having a history of cancer, the discovery of the disease is something that is supposed to happen to others. In my family, there was no history of this disease. When the doctor confirmed I had testicular cancer, I was surprised. "How did this happen?"

The first suggestion of cancer emerged through self-examination. I had noticed an enlargement in one of my testicles. As a male, I easily brushed it off as nothing to worry about. "Maybe it was a passing infection," I thought. More plausible, I explained it as a testosterone spurt normal during midlife.

I was wrong on both counts. After two months, I finally conceded my self-diagnosis was incorrect and a doctor's visit might be warranted. I dropped my pants and raised my hopes the situation was not too serious.

Cancer, however, is always a serious matter. The early stages for me were the most fearful, not knowing what the presence of cancer might mean. The term cancer conjured up images of suffering and death. As an adult, I had few friends and relatives who had been diagnosed with cancer; but now, it was not the other. "*I have cancer*" resounded in my mind as if hearing someone else's voice.

The first ultrasound exam revealed the presence of a tumor. The technician was having a slow day, and he allowed me to watch the monitor as he rolled a small apparatus on my private parts. Seeing myself on the screen, I felt beside myself.

The doctor noted the results and ordered further studies to confirm the findings.

The second technician maintained a more professional distance, probably because of the intimate examination she had to perform on a male. With stoic demeanor, she announced it was time to get naked which I correctly assumed she meant me and not her. I smiled and waived at the camera, knowing it was show time. I was no longer embarrassed. I resigned myself that my private parts were no longer private.

The examination appeared routine until the technician made an abrupt stop and raced out the room without explanation. Five minutes, ten minutes, no word. The room was dim and quiet, my body in compliant spread-eagle position, my mind beginning to drift into plausible scenarios. "What did the technician see? What caused her to dart from the room with haste?"

Hispanics are rich in their religious traditions. Sacred images have appeared on trees, windows, bathroom walls, even tortillas. "This would be a first," I thought,"What if she saw...?" "Sacrilegious, don't even go there," I argued with myself. The mental image dissipated as the doctor walked in.

The tumor was confirmed. The doctor identified it as cancerous, aggressive, and malignant. It could spread if it were to find entry into the lymphatic system. Cancer could end up in any part of my body, the organs, even the brain. Surgery was scheduled within days, with no time to process the news and implications of this invasive creature within.

I never felt pain and only occasional discomfort. This did not conform to the gravity of the case the doctor was describing. This is a young man's concern, usually affecting males 15-37. I was already 50, so I thought perhaps the doctor had misdiagnosed me or confused the charts with a young man in the other cubicle. My denial was still playing in my mind. The images, however, did not lie; and I conceded to the reality that I had cancer.

Surgery was routine, with no complications. It was routine for the doctor, but certainly not for me. I had no previous experience with this. As an outpatient, I was released in six hours, in time to stop for lunch on the way home. I do not know what was in the anesthesia because I woke up with a strong craving for Chinese food.

Fortunately, the cancer was confined, with no signs of having spread to other parts of the body. No chemotherapy was needed, but 30 rounds of radiation were ordered as prevention.

Cancer, however, is peculiar. It may resurface with a different face, in a manner as before—unexpected and intrusive. The next experience may not be as kind.

I still wonder how testicular cancer became part of my life. I have no answer. Life is like that.

CHAPTER 12

The Hot Streets

"TAKE OFF YOUR SHOES. Remove your socks. Ready?" The competition began as soon as our bare soles hit the street. On summer days the streets were hot, volcanic hot, especially as the black tar softened and bubbled like molten lava. The gravel was embedded in the tar, absorbing the heat and magnifying the temperature far beyond the 100-degree weather.

Newcomers to the sport seldom lasted. Their feet bounced back to the curb upon first contact with the pavement. They quit quickly, failing to see merit in this character-building activity.

The veterans meanwhile demonstrated techniques from experience: a slow shift from ball to heel, a slight wiggle from side-to-side, and an intermittent tiptoe to allow the rest of the foot to catch a breath. Participants stood stone-faced, only allowing a subtle grimace to camouflage the pain. We were the coal-walkers of the day, enduring the flaming streets with courage.

Our feet toughened with time, and the competition evolved into a walk-a-thon. We targeted the public library as our destination, a grueling eight blocks on the sizzling pavement. No one ever made it without a break, but the aim was to endure a little longer than our competitor. In the end, no one really cared who won, and the consolation was in arriving at the library where we could recuperate prior to our return home—with our shoes on.

Perhaps the boredom of summer had set in. Perhaps it was just a guy thing, being all boys in the family. I do not know who came up with the idea, maybe not even from the brothers. I anticipated some grand life lesson or some nugget of wisdom to emerge from our experience. Nothing profound has surfaced so far.

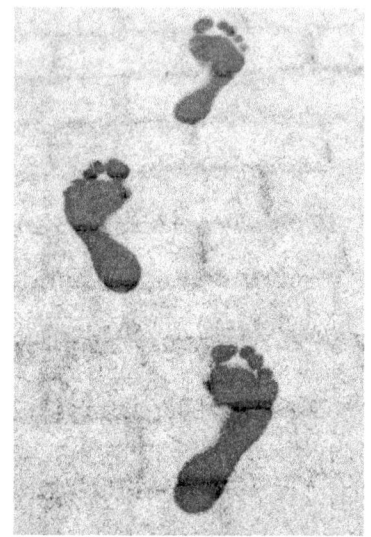

Perhaps it was just the fun of the moment, recalling how we scorched and blistered our tender youthful feet. Perhaps it was how we endured the pain and torture of the melted tar. Perhaps it was how we absorbed the sharp edges and protrusions of the embedded rocks into our naked soles.

Yes, it must have been the fun of the moment.

CHAPTER 13

The Bread Controversy

THE CROWD WAS SPARSE, a distinct advantage when in line at a cafeteria. People were not behind us glancing at their watches and grunting with impatience trying to get the line to move faster. We could take our time and appreciate the full array of food.

The salads were a feast in themselves, an artful arrangement of fruits, vegetables, dressings, and toppings—an exquisite spread that could make a carnivore salivate. I relished the visual display of salads, but I skipped to the main entrees while my cousin moved ahead more decisively. This was her home town, and this must have been her regular eatery as she picked her food with robotic selection.

To complete her order, she scanned the breads. "I'll have a roll," she insisted; and to which I added "I'll take a bun." That triggered a conversation which dominated our visit. We had not seen each other for years, and we focused our conversation on bread!

"What is the difference," we began, "between a roll and a bun?" Was it the texture, the shape, the way it was baked, or the ingredients? Was it the dough, the kneading process, or was it left to the discretion of the baker? We entertained every angle, every plausible explanation; but we stalemated with no conclusion.

We looked for a person of knowledge, one to enlighten us on these burning questions. We had no access to the internet; and we knew our minds would not rest until we resolved the matter.

We paid the cashier and presented her with our dilemma, asking her to bring enlightenment to our unsettled issue.

"With your many years of experience working in the restaurant business, can you please tell us the difference between a roll and a bun? We have been debating this for over an hour and we have found no reasonable explanation."

The cashier paused thoughtfully for a moment, looked at her cash register, and responded with confidence. "Two cents." We left the cafeteria, and no more was said on the subject.

CHAPTER 14

The Colonoscopy

SOME THINGS ARE INEVITABLE when you are a child—those first shots or vaccines, the trip to the dentist, and eating repulsive vegetables parents insist are good for you.

Today, a dental trip is not as threatening. In the dark days of dentistry when we were growing up, grueling images flooded the imagination the night before the appointment. Equipment was not as sophisticated; the procedures were intimidating. Oversized hands explored the contours of your mouth—jabbing, poking, tapping, picking, scraping—and this was just preliminary. The drill was reminiscent of a sci-fi movie, the motor rumbling like a rotor saw in horror scenes when the maniacal doctor would chop up the corpse.

Somehow, we survived those inevitable situations as children. As adults we moved into a different set of the inevitable.

The doctor's visit was routine—the annual exam, no particular complaint being presented. Then, as if in slow motion, the doctor's lips quivered and the hideous word slipped out with echoing articulation, "c-o-l-o-n-o-s-c-o-p-y."

I had never had the experience and I knew it was coming some day. I had heard the term around the water cooler, usually within the soft-core humor males embellished about their personal checkups—prostate exams, turn-and-cough experiences, and other tales of intimate probings. The stories and jokes are funny when they are directed to someone else. Now it was my turn.

The doctor began to describe the procedure, and this was helpful because my only images were the ones prescribed by friends' experiences. In an effort to be polite and not be too graphic, the doctor began to gesture how a camera would be inserted into my body to take pictures. This escalated my fear. .

First, it was the unknown that stirred anxiety; now we were venturing into what I did know. I envisioned MY camera equipment. My lens was 10 inches long and 3 inches wide. "So, Doctor, you are going to do what!" Sparked by a flash of imagination, a moment of hysteria set in. My rational self caught up with my emotions and I calmed as the doctor clarified. He assured me I would feel nothing since I would be under anesthesia. This brought some comfort, knowing I would not be awake to suffer from this highly invasive procedure.

The anesthesia worked better than expected; and I drifted into total blackout within seconds. I awakened with no discomfort, no sensation, and not a sliver of memory of the procedure. My first thought was on the doctor, hoping that he had taken some remarkable shots so we would not have to reschedule another photo shoot.

I look back and have often wondered what would inspire anyone to go into this field. In school, I never recall anyone talking about this field on career day. In any case, I concluded it was a necessary profession and doctors responded to a personal calling. I came to appreciate what they do. They had probed and discovered my inner beauty, declaring me cleared until my next scheduled meeting in 10 years.

I did not savor the experience in the moment, but now I felt credentialed to contribute to the water cooler humor—a bit crude, a little too explicit, but a badge of honor having survived one of the inevitable passages of adulthood.

CHAPTER 15

Lost Tradition

THEY SAY DINOSAURS and man did not co-exist. I was there; I saw them. They say dragons were only a fantasy. They were real, and I attest to their existence. They say monsters were a childhood imagination, but I saw them all the time.

As children, especially on a slothful afternoon of summer, we lay on the grass and gazed into the sky. Clouds—cirrus, cumulus, nimbus, and a few others we could never remember—swept by at different altitudes. Cumulus were majestic, fluffy, and expansive. They floated along, ever shifting and combining with others. They were my favorite. They were dominant and strong, yet with a soft and gentle side to them.

We envisioned characters from books and comics; but most of the time, monsters, animals, and people emerged, the clouds constantly being shaped by the changing winds. Among friends, each fought for the other's attention. "Look, there's a cowboy riding a dragon," and the other would respond "but look over there, can you see…?"

Of course, there was alway one of the neighborhood friends who was clueless. "Where? I do not see it. Where's the dragon?" By then, the dragon had lost its tail, and now it was a two-headed goat butting a kid in the rear.

Cloud watching was a common experience for generations. It helped develop imagination. It taught us to entertain ourselves when we were bored. It taught socialization with friends; and on occasion, it taught us patience with the clueless one among us. Our fantasies flourished. Our minds ventured into territories that could never be experienced in real life. In one sense, it was an escape; on the other hand, it was an appreciation of life in the moment. We did not see it that way as children. It was just a distraction during the day, finding fun in the small things of life. That's what children did.

Gazing into the clouds has become a lost art for children.

Fantasies have been replaced by video games and movies. Computer graphics created by others have replaced the personal imagination of individuals.

Today, I still look to the clouds. Occasionally, I still see the fantasies of childhood. The monsters remain; the funny faces continue to stir a smile within me. Most of the time, I just see clouds; and I wonder if I have lost a critical part of self going into adulthood.

CHAPTER 16

Bad Hair Day

LIGHTING FROM THE NORTH window distorted my appearance; or perhaps I had not noticed how my hair had grayed so much. It did not matter because I was between jobs, no one to impress. "What a great time to experiment," I thought. "Why not color my hair and return to the image of youthful days? I will see if my wife notices when she returns from work."

I went to the store to purchase a do-it-yourself kit. How difficult can it be splashing and rinsing a little color on my head? I had seen many commercials, and it looked simple. I entered the aisle of hair products and was overwhelmed by the hundreds of options. "I need to look confident," I thought, "and go straight for the product."

I practiced the line, "This is for my wife." I was self-conscious and did not want to give the impression to others that it was for me. I had always associated coloring one's hair with women. Fortunately, no one approached me and asked me if I needed help. My rehearsal was not needed, and I breathed relief as I quickly slipped into the next shopping aisle.

I purchased the black hair dye, thinking back to my younger days in high school. I looked at the picture of the girl on the box and projected the male equivalent in my head. "Maybe when I finish, they will put me on a box."

I proceeded slowly ensuring uniform coverage. I worked the color into the scalp and waited the prescribed time. In fact, I decided to keep it on 10 more minutes to make sure the color had really taken. "Just in case," I thought.

I waited with great excitement and then quickly rinsed my hair. I towel-dried, rushed to the mirror, and saw my smile of elevated anticipation sink to a horrified shock.

I rushed to the packaging and ensured I had purchased *black.* I did not know black came in so many shades. On a scale of 1-10, this black was a 30, darker than a black cat at midnight during a lunar eclipse.

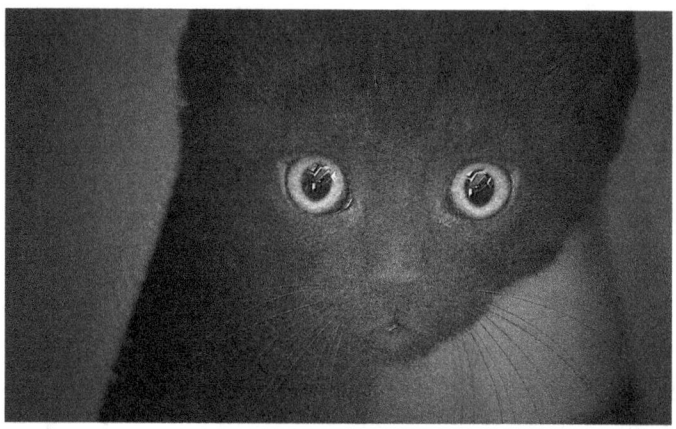

"What now?" as I slipped down the slope of panic and depression. I washed my hair five times with no effect. I reached for the peroxide as I had heard it was used to lighten hair. No help. In desperation, I read the instructions. Even worse, it clearly stated, "Do not use peroxide." Lesson one learned: "Read all directions before proceeding." It must be a male thing.

I called the 1-800 number on the box and was advised that with multiple washings—no number specified—my hair should return to normal. What did that mean—a week, a month, next year? Panic was rumbling in my stomach. I waited for my wife, now hoping she would NOT notice. As she entered the house, her face exploded with greater shock than mine. Between subdued chuckles, she offered a series of suggestions—all of which I had tried, including the peroxide.

In desperation, she blurted out we must find a salon still open at this late hour. She parked at the mall, and I followed her at a cautious distance to hide my embarrassment. She entered a hair salon and inquired very calmly, "I have a FRIEND who…" At this point, I poked my coal-colored head from around the pillar and showed my face. Now she had to admit her friend was actually her husband, and we all laughed—easier for them as shades of red flushed my face.

"Time cures everything," they said; and no new advice was given but to just wait it out. As I slithered out the store, I could almost hear the stylist rolling in laughter and exclaiming to her fellow workers, "You get what you pay for."

Worry and panic consumed me. I had a job interview in three days; and other than shave my head, I had no alternatives. I felt like the young teen walking into class with his first pimple, feeling as if everyone in the room was staring at the small eruption on his face. For me, it was like having Mount Vesuvius. No one could miss this spectacle. I prepared to have a parade of stares from the office staff, especially as I passed the receptionist.

Women notice everything, and they are not hesitant to relish in the stylish mishaps of others. I walked in, nevertheless, with head held high. I interviewed and I got the job. I do not know if the hair had any influence on my selection, but I secretly entertained the idea I must have stood out from the other candidates.

Eventually, my hair returned to its original color exactly as the 1-800 number had promised—"eventually" being two months. The grays emerged again, and I embraced them with the same jubilation as the biblical father welcomed his prodigal son.

Some say gray hairs are a sign of wisdom; others claim they are just a sign of aging. I concluded the latter as being more precise as wisdom was clearly absent, not a to be found in this calamity.

CHAPTER 17

History Lost

ONE HUNDRED SIXTY THOUSAND allied troops stormed the beaches of Normandy on June 6. Seventy-three thousand were American. My father was one of them—the year, 1944. A reported 29,000 Americans were killed in the Normandy invasion which raged over several months, another 106,000 wounded or missing. My father was one of the fortunate ones who made it home, a significant event considering I would not be here otherwise.

World War II for us as children was a history lesson at school. We learned about countries, leaders, battles, and dates—all information for a test but with little to no interest in our lives. I did not appreciate that my father was part of that history, a soldier in the Army in the European campaign.

He spoke little about the war, never bringing it up on his own. He kept his box of medals and patches corresponding with his service in Europe. He never explained what they were for or how he had earned them. He also brought home several memorabilia including a few ammunition boxes, a German Luger, and a Swastika flag. We did not realize the importance or value of these items. As kids, we often draped the flag over the clothesline, made a tent, and we camped overnight with friends in the backyard. I was surprised that police or neighbors driving by the house did not report any suspicion upon seeing the Swastika in the yard.

Our mother shared little as well. She showed us a box of letters she had received from our dad during the war. As children, we were more interested in the stamps, like the 3-cent victory stamp, that were on the envelopes as we all had our collections. Our mother related how our dad would lunge under the table when he heard a plane overhead.

I imagine this was not unusual for many who had experienced enemy bombers, especially when our dad told us how he had lost many companions during the war.

We never asked to hear his war stories and he never offered to reminisce, even after decades. For him, the war was an event of the past to be categorized and sealed. For many soldiers, the memories of war remained unspoken.

As an adult now and years after his death, I wish I had probed into his experiences of the war—basic information such as where he had trained, where he had been stationed overseas, and what his experience was as a soldier in World War II.

I believe that with time, he would have spoken personally about his companions, his missions, his encounters in battle, and his loss of friends. I do not think he would have been able to share all that he had witnessed as he had lost many who were around him. It would have been a sensitive subject even decades after the war.

Now I can say that I would like to have heard about Normandy from a first-hand perspective. However, as a child, his history was not a topic of importance. I saw him as "dad" and my focus was on my own interests. I can see now how much I missed—not just about the war but about his life experiences as a child, growing up, early life, and later. Now I wish I could fill the vacuum from all that was lost, but it is too late. Although some stories were passed on, they will never fill my craving to know more.

Some regrets will never be appeased.

CHAPTER 18

Sharing

THEY SAY IGNORANCE is bliss; and as children, there was an abundance of bliss in all of us. We did not worry about contamination or sharing of germs. We were friends, and we did not even consider sanitation or food safety issues.

Today, we hear about the 3-second rule; but in those days, there was no rule. If by chance a cookie would fall on the ground, we would pick it up and consume it. Of course, we did take some precautions. We brushed the cookie with our hands to knock off any germs. We were practical, certainly not wasteful, and it seemed to work every time.

Smelly, dirty, and sweaty were something we all had in common after a neighborhood football game. If anyone had loose change, sharing a Coke became a communal ritual. The one who purchased had rights to the first sip, but then the bottle made the rounds. We shared fairly among the 4-5 guys.

Some of the guys were crude, obviously void of any manners. They would drink shamelessly from the bottle with their slobbering lips and then pass it to the next guy. No one ever commented on their barbaric gestures; some things we could overlook. A little backwash or drool never hurt any of us. This was my first awareness of social etiquette, the differences in upbringing among friends. The rest of us at least had the decency of wiping the Coke bottle with our sweaty sleeve before sharing.

No one remembers anybody getting sick in those years from sipping on a shared Coke or from finishing a cookie that had fallen on the ground. Today, the germ climate has changed. The commercial industry has capitalized on this fear of contamination and has marketed every type of spray, gel, lotion, powder, and mist to sterilize the environment.

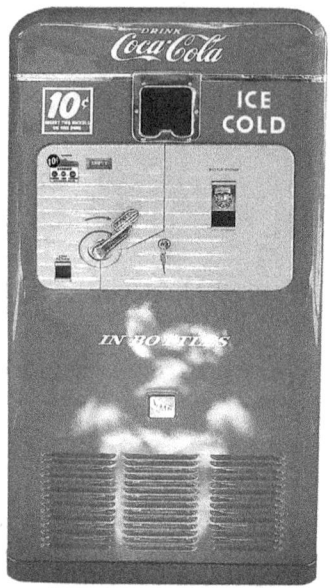

Our method as kids ignored contamination issues. We shared openly with each other and built our immune systems. Whatever it was, it worked. We grew up healthy. If only we could have packaged our formula and marketed it to the masses today!

CHAPTER 19

The Headstone

THE FIELD LOOKED LIKE any other, except for minor evidence the earth had been disturbed in places. The ground was uneven and grass was clumped in mounds, all overgrown with an occasional open patch. I searched for a sign of recent activity—a marker, a sunken section of earth, a small mound, a metal stake. It was the paupers' cemetery. There was no sense of permanency, unlike the adjacent field which was manicured and orderly.

The young woman I brought with me had lost her husband several months prior, and she had come to lay a headstone. The deceased man was forty years older, but he had taken care of her. He had gained companionship in his elderly years to this young woman. The least she could do was to provide a marked stone as evidence of his life.

"I think it was by this tree," she said in Spanish. "Maybe closer to this bush." There were several spots that suggested a burial in recent months. With no certainty, she conceded a spot and laid the headstone in her husband's honor. He had no known family except for his wife of a few years.

She yielded a moment of silence at the presumed grave and signaled a quiet good-bye, probably her last before she returned to her native Mexico. I do not remember any tears, but that is not to say she felt no grief. Even with a difference in age, she had developed a bond beyond companionship, a genuine caring for the elderly man. She radiated a deep love for him.

His grave marker was the only one in the paupers' site. He likely will never have visitors except for the occasional curiosity seeker who thrills in reading tombstone epitaphs. The man left few possessions. He left no legacy to be remembered. He was dead; and in this sense, he had gained equality with everyone around him, even with those who had been buried in the opulent section of the cemetery.

Dying is one tradition no one escapes; and I do not plan to break with tradition. I suspect I will die in old age, only because I tend to procrastinate. I have not decided on burial or cremation, but I have ruled out taxidermy.

We attend funerals to bid farewell to family and friends who have passed, and to mingle and reminisce with those who are still with us. We always promise more reunions to appreciate each other before it is too late. We always remind each other at the next funeral of this promise we made at the last. It has become part of the ritual.

Funerals remind us of our mortality, serving as a premonition of our passing some day. By that time, our lives will have been defined on how we had patterned our life. Hopefully, we will tilt more on the positive side on the balance of good and evil.

Unfortunately, much of our human spirit is consumed on things of no importance. I witnessed an infuriated man who approached the counter at McDonalds. He threw his food, complaining in raised voice how his order had been filled incorrectly. Similarly, at another restaurant the following week, a man at a buffet hunted down the manager to voice his anger because they had stopped serving cinnamon rolls. His irate state of mind led him to me, thinking I was the manager; and he initiated his rant of anger and threats.

"Do you know how much my buddies and I bring to this restaurant each week? You know, we can go somewhere else to spend our money." I listened with empathy to his complaint which softened his tone; but then I had to inform him I did not work there. The manager, in a similar shirt as mine, was standing by the buffet line. He approached and calmed the customer and offered to make a new batch of cinnamon rolls for his group. Life was good again.

I do not criticize too harshly because I could easily contribute personal examples of my volatility and pettiness. Stories like this are common, with incidents at work, school, home, and even at church. Life is short, and this is how we manage it.

Funerals refocus my spirit, reminding me my days are numbered and the count is spiraling toward the finish line. My breaths will cease and my heart will generate its last tick. My mouth will utter its last word—much relief to many. My limbs will succumb to stillness. My complaints and concerns will dissolve to nothingness; and in the end, my body will become one with the earth.

But I am not there yet; and I find no urgency. Meanwhile, those of us who remain face life with each other until that next funeral calls our number. I cannot alter the life of others, but I can do my part by embracing a spirit that dignifies and respects each person who sojourns with me, even if only for a passing and seemingly insignificant moment.

I aspire to rise above the lures of life rooted in pettiness. Some days I am successful; other days I am not. Life is like that.

CHAPTER 20

The Hunted

THE WOMAN CHARGED down the road like a bull from Pamplona. There was no mistake; she was headed toward us. "Are you shooting these?" she yelled, obviously furious as she opened her hand to show a steel ball the size of a marble.

White wing and dove season had just opened, and we had stationed ourselves near an open field. The woman's house was a block away, and she described how this object had rained from the sky and pelted her back as she sat on the porch.

We had shotguns—my father and two brothers did—and the woman presumed it had come from us. Anyone with a shotgun would know pellets were tiny and nothing compared to the marble-sized projectile she produced. Its round shape resembled no bullet from any known firearm.

Not convinced of our innocence since we were the only hunters in the area, the woman stormed back to her house without further argument. I shuffled to the rear of the car where I secretly disposed of my slingshot. I never would have believed I could shoot the distance to her house, but the evidence proved otherwise. I recognized the projectile, a ball bearing I had loaded in my slingshot. I felt criminal, especially in my cowardly disposal of the weapon. I kept my silence, still stunned in disbelief.

We continued the hunt, and I retired the slingshot for the rest of the day. The woman had left with my last piece of ammo, and I certainly was not going to reclaim it. I consigned myself to retrieving the birds for my father and brothers. I cleaned the game, plucking the feathers, pulling the heads off, and removing the embedded pellets from the birds.

I had nothing to show for my day of hunting except the memories of hitting the woman. I did not have the guts to tell her that I had been the one to blame, not only shooting her but shooting her in the back. A part of me also chuckled at the experience. What were the odds of hitting a woman a block away! She had charged down the road like a wild buffalo; and in my warped mind of the moment, I felt like a big-game hunter. She was my trophy.

I am sure the woman retreated to her house, and the ball bearing became a topic of conversation for weeks among her family and friends. She likely embellished the story for her listeners—how she was on death's doorstep. "Two inches to the right and it would have severed my spinal cord; and my poor children would have been traumatized in finding my sprawled body on the ground." In telling the story, timing would have to be perfect: a short pause, a dainty dab to the eyes, a soft-spoken sigh. "I am lucky to be here with you today."

Among my family and friends, the woman remained a topic of conversation, not for months but for years. Every hunting trip triggered the story; events between hunting trips triggered the story. Repeating it did not diminish the excitement nor the humor of the event imprinted in our memories. No embellishment was needed. Her image charging down the road made the bulls of Pamplona look like a petting zoo.

Sometimes, bad things happen but they make great stories at a later time. This one left an impression on me, but probably not as much as it left an impression on the woman.

CHAPTER 21

Heavy Issues

A POUND PER YEAR seems negligible, the weight gain imperceptible. It may have been the extra enchilada at the office luncheon, the irresistible 2-for-1 special, or that one-more-visit to the all-you-can-eat buffet. All seems harmless until that pound per year occurs over three decades.

As much as I enjoy eating, 30 pounds was hard to swallow. "The scale must be defective," I thought, "or perhaps it needed to be recalibrated." I never had problems with the scale until we started outsourcing our manufacturing to foreign countries.

A visit to the doctor's office for my annual checkup landed me on one of those old-fashioned scales. The base was heavy

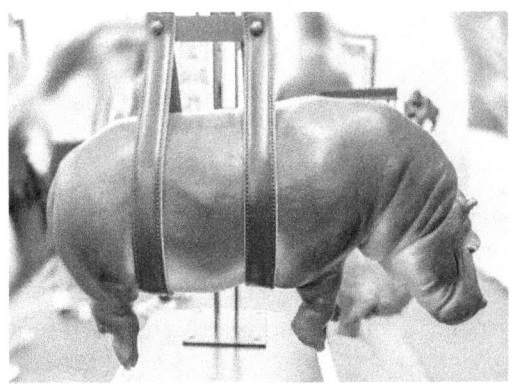

and stable, capable of weighing a hippo if needed. I was hoping that was not the reason the nurse directed me to it in place of the digital scale in the corner. She set the base weight and began to slide the measure along the top bar.

I welcomed the familiar apparatus, and I felt confident it would assess my corporal mass more accurately. I related to the nurse that my scale at home showed me to be 30 pounds overweight. She smiled as she scanned my body from head to toe. "You are probably right. Your scale may need to be recalibrated," commenting with a tone of empathy but her subtle smile hinting of sarcasm.

The nurse maneuvered the measure along the top bar—a few notches, a few more, finally stretching to the end—and the scale did not balance. I knew what that meant, and images of the hippo began to return. She scribbled my vitals on the chart and escorted me to the nearest cubicle. Her smile returned but her sarcasm emerged with much less subtlety.

Twenty minutes of waiting for the doctor seemed like hours. I was alone in my thoughts, still stunned I was 35 pounds overweight. The original 30 pounds sounded more appealing. I could not reconcile my mental image of self with the scale readings.

I recalled the distortion mirrors at the carnival. As children, we would roar with laughter in front of those panels which disfigured our images as we jumped up and down waving our arms—our bodies changing from scrawny to fat, from tall to short, from straight to twisted, and through an endless array of facial expressions. When we tired of this, we would walk away fully intact as ourselves—leaving the distortions behind. Now, however, I had become those distortions. I was the image in the mirror. The fat walked away with me.

The doctor still had not arrived. My worry escalated, wondering what other surprises might emerge with my lab work. Finally the nurse and the doctor entered. My mind immediately ventured into the worst scenario. Why would it take two to share the news about me? Was I terminal?

With professional stature, the doctor began to spew numbers foreign to my understanding. "What does all that mean?" I questioned but I really did not want to hear.

The doctor summarized. "Your blood pressure is pre-hypertensive, your sugar is pre-diabetic, your weight is pre-obesity, and your cholesterol is borderline or pre-elevated." The report left me pre-occupied, too much to handle at one time. I found some consolation that the doctor could share the results with me pre-mortem.

A week later, I reviewed the results. I looked in the mirror and still saw myself as normal. Fat was the other guy sitting in the doctor's office or the one at the restaurant gorging on a tower of pancakes and sausages swimming in a pool of syrup. Fat was everyone else but me.

Weight gain had been slow, and so the incremental increases went unnoticed. "After all," I reasoned, "I maintained the same pants size for years," overlooking that like many males, I could flip my belly bulge over my waistline. I was in denial and considered my weight as normal for my age.

The weight gain was evident in subtle ways. It produced the guttural grunt when bending to tie my shoes. It was the extra gasp for air when climbing stairs. It was the sucking in of the gut in order to clasp the pants at the waist. It was the inability to toss, only turn, when trying to sleep. It was the inability to jump out of bed, only roll. With time, it all seemed normal. As we get older, we are more forgiving of self and blame it on age.

The doctor's visit served as a wake-up call to address my health more seriously. Occasionally, I still go for the 2-for-1 specials and indulge in buffets. The fat cells still frequent my body, but I consider them as visitors and not as permanent residents. I still have some cells which have overstayed their welcome.

I have not been lured into becoming vegetarian or vegan. Being a herbivore seems incompatible with being human. I refrain from fad diets; and I avoid "magic pills" that advertise

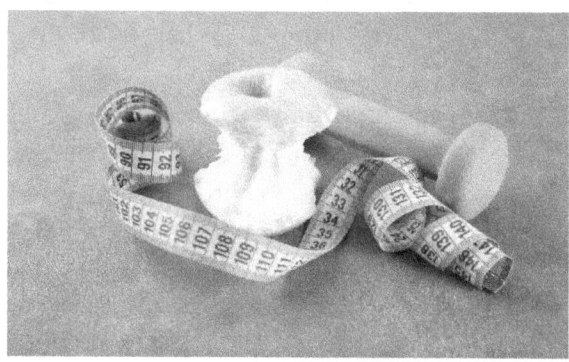

losing weight by doing no exercise while continuing old eating patterns.

Motivation seems to be the key factor, and I think of family and friends in making healthy choices. I want to be around a little longer so I can be with them—and hopefully the feelings will be mutual.

CHAPTER 22

Obituaries

AT A CERTAIN AGE—one will know when it comes—the news and sports sections of the newspaper cede their importance. The relevant news are found in the obituaries.

As a child, I often thought the obituaries were reserved for old people. Anyone who looked like an adult—anyone over 30—was old. As an altar boy, I served many funerals and all the deceased fit that description.

Being young, I did not understand but I eventually discovered death had no age requirements. Pictures of newborns and children found their places in the obituaries. The concept of death remained vague and mysterious, but I realized that I was not immune.

Children died and that meant that as a child, I also could die. Nevertheless, I felt safe because death occurred in other families. Eventually, this understanding changed as relatives began to occupy the lists of the deceased. Death was getting closer as it began to show its face more clearly.

Now as an adult, death has been a frequent visitor on my life's journey. No longer the stranger, no longer the distant relative, death had come to many friends, classmates, and work companions. It had come to immediate family. Death was no longer a stranger who beckoned others, who was searching the community for the next one on the list. Death had become a companion with me. I am on that list, and I await the tap on the shoulder to alert me of my time.

I plan to insert my own obituary. The standard ones are sterile, describing everyone as "loving, faithful, compassionate, full of zeal for life, and who will be missed by family, children, and friends."

Work history and accomplishments are often mentioned, perhaps to garner admiration. Some prepare for death, building their legacy to establish immortal memories for subsequent generations. Some attach their names to monuments, buildings, plaques, foundations, and streets to perpetuate their existence among the living.

I venture towards simplicity; a few words will suffice.

"I loved the best I could, especially my family. Sometimes I was successful in sharing that love; other times I fell short. I had many acquaintances along the road of life, some who merited to be called friend. I was honored to have shared the road for a brief passing with them; and I hope our relationship shared moments of enjoyment and mutual appreciation. My family knows my love; my God knows my heart."

Nothing else needs to be published. My body will lay in the coffin for viewing, manicured to a degree never attained in life.

People like to comment on how good someone looks—as if that really mattered at this point. I considered a provision in my will to have my eyes altered—much like those museum pieces of art in which the eyes follow the viewer from every angle. That might create a stir in the line, entertainment for the mischievous but scandalous among the traditional mourners. My wife knows me too well, and she will probably elect to have a closed casket to avoid disruption.

At the funeral, I will be an anonymous person to the altar server—just another funeral to which he had been assigned. He likely will have had little experience with death, much like I had at that young age. My presence will suggest to him that obituaries and funerals are only for the old, people over 30.

I am at peace with that, knowing he is only beginning his journey of life. Eventually he will understand his own mortality.

The time will come; he will know. For now, the innocence of childhood should be respected and preserved.

CHAPTER 23

Naming Your Child

OVER 7 BILLION PEOPLE in the world and each has a name. It should be easy to choose one, but selecting the *right name* adds difficulty to the process. It is no longer the name of a child; it is the name of *my child.*

No "juniors" for sure. He likely will be called "junior" for the rest of his life, and his real name would never be used. Our son deserved his own identity, and one that was clear. Life is also too short to perpetually explain the uniqueness of a name. "Hi, my name is Ptomaz, you know like Thomas, but the P is silent and it ends with a Z and not an S."

"Keep it simple," we reminded ourselves, "and avoid nicknames." I never understood how "William" converted to "Bill" or how "Bobby" came out of "Robert." If parents wanted a Bill, why name him William? Selecting a name for our child was becoming overly-complicated.

Out in public, my wife felt a sudden flush of fluid, and in a slight panic, she announced her water bag had broken. This was my first experience with this, and I had no idea how much time we had. I feared the baby would slip out unexpectedly. Movie scenes always made it look easy—with a few pushes, groans, and final excruciating grunts, the baby emerges. The mother sighs with relief, the couple smiles and hugs, a few tears are shed, and everyone celebrates.

I did not want to play the movie role. I was not confident my experience would have the Hollywood ending. Fortunately, we arrived at the hospital with time. Contractions became more frequent; and four hours later, our son arrived. With no complications in the delivery, the Hollywood script kicked in and the hugs and celebrations began.

The nurse entered the room quietly. "You may get ready and go home with your child, but first we need to register a name. I'm sure you have the perfect name for this perfect child."

"No problem, give us a few minutes," we responded with confidence. Our blank stares displayed our honest response. Nine months of expecting and we still had not selected a name. I felt another round of labor pains as we fumbled with the task.

The nurse entered again, more emphatic than before, and announced the need to vacate the room. Patients were waiting outside, and her patience could wait no longer. Pressures increased to finalize a name for the birth certificate. Like a buffet,

there were so many choices but we could not decide. In desperation, we grabbed the telephone directory and skimmed the columns of names, page after page, city after city.

It was easy to reject some of the options such as Commodore, Edgardo, and Chauncey—boys' names appropriate for children in another time and setting. I had no plan to make them fashionable again with my son. It was excruciatingly difficult to choose the right name. Faithful to our original guidelines, we kept it simple, easy, and clear—nothing unusual, with easy spelling and pronunciation; and we proudly selected the name of Mark.

The nurse reacted with her scripted lines reserved for all parents. "That's a wonderful name and congratulations on a beautiful child." We smiled and accepted her routine remarks and complemented them with our own surge of joy that can only be appreciated by the parents of a newborn.

"But before you leave," the nurse quickly interjected, "Is that Mark with a K or a C?"

CHAPTER 24

Fear of Night

AS CHILDREN, WE ALL harbored fears—snakes, thunderstorms, monsters, the dark. It was a natural part of growing up. Boys were no exception. They would confess to the first three, but they were always in denial about being fearful of the dark. No one wanted to be called "sissy" or "scaredy cat." Even children had their pride.

We had seen too many horror shows, and treacherous events always occurred at night. We were impressionable—our minds convincing us there were no reasons to fear, our emotions arguing to the contrary. Walking home from a friend's house stirred memories of the movies. During the day, the four blocks would have passed as uneventful. The darkness, however, brought new concerns.

Night had set, and my senses were on optimum alert. My Catholic school training kicked in, provoking a litany of prayers for protection. No images of God, warrior angels, or patron saints entered my mind—only flashbacks of horror scenes from movies.

Shadows flickered around me, producing shapes and figures grasping at my body. The wind bristled through the branches creaking with eerie tempo while an errant dog barked blindly toward a row of hedges. "I'm being watched, maybe followed," I wondered in quivering thought.

The dog sensed someone…or something. A crackling noise in the bushes erupted like a branch snapping underfoot. Glimmers of light shown through the bushes, two eyes staring my way, no semblance of being human. The dog had charged into the brush and made no exit. Shadows and silence erupted with thunderous impact.

My steps accelerated to a quickened pace, a nervous trot, and a final dash to the front door of the house—the shadows trailing close behind. I made it home *this* time, but I gained no confidence for the next time.

Daylight always returned the neighborhood to normal, providing temporary relief to my terrors. I could not attest whether imagination had overtaken me or whether the dark had sought me as prey. I searched the bushes and could find no hints of disturbance or any explanation for the shimmering eyes staring at me.

It must have been my imagination with a play of shadows, noises, and visual distortions. Yes, it *was* my imagination filled with mental trickery, runaway images, and perceptions of childhood. My reasoning began to kick in. I had no cause to fear—although the dog was never seen again.

CHAPTER 25

Altar Boy

AS A MALE IN CATHOLIC SCHOOL, some things could not be avoided. Fourth grade was the year of recruitment to be an altar boy. This was not considered just an obligation but an honor. Altar boy was gender specific as girls were not allowed to serve in this capacity.

Becoming an altar boy was not automatic nor was it simple. Mass was in Latin, and showing proficiency was a prerequisite. "*Introibo ad altar Dei*," the priest would begin each Mass; and we responded accordingly, "*ad Deum qui laetificat iuventutum meum.*"

Responses became easier with practice; and we practiced religiously, even playing Mass at the house to learn the rituals. We were innocent, using juice and Kool-Aid for wine and smashed bread for Communion.

The experience introduced a new vocabulary—still used today—and it was necessary to learn in case the priest sent us quickly to retrieve an item during Mass. These were useful terms in a Scrabble game with non-Catholics. None of them had heard of "pall, burse, maniple, cincture, censor, or thurible." Words like pyx used highly-valued letters, especially on a triple word score.

First time use of these words always brought a challenge by opponents; but they soon learned the legitimacy of words from the Catholic pool. They ceased the challenges, and this allowed the insertion of fake words with our gullible friends. "*Malix*, good for triple letter on the 'x' and double word score. You know *malix,* the special vestment the Pope wears when he is first elected and sits on the throne of Peter." It sounded feasible to friends ignorant of Catholic ways, and I figured I could always settle the score in confession.

The Catholic culture was always strange to people of other faiths, especially noticeable during a funeral when a mix from other churches gathered. Catholics would dip their hands in holy water as they entered the church. During the Mass, they genuflected, sat, stood, knelt, stood again, made the sign of the cross, made special symbols on the forehead, mouth, and chest, bowed, and then stood and knelt again, and genuflected on the way out.

The Catholics knew the gestures had meaning and symbolism—not always understood but faithfully practiced. The non-Catholics remained in stupor in their Mass confusion; and they found it easier to sit on the benches in silence to observe the ritual drama.

The Church has witnessed many changes over the decades. Church services are in the native language instead of Latin, but Catholics still engage in the prayerful gymnastics during the Mass. Girls have joined the ranks of altar servers alongside the boys. Non-Catholics still look at Catholics with wariness; and

Catholics still chuckle at non-Catholics with amusement as they appear lost during a funeral or wedding.

Many of my Catholic friends have chosen other paths since those early days of Catholic school. Others have continued faithful to their roots of origin. We have scattered like seeds planted by the wind. Life is like that.

CHAPTER 26

Days of Old

MY GRANDFATHER WAS always old. His whitened hair, trimmed mustache, slowed gait, and wire-rimmed spectacles completed his profile. He carried a grandfatherly image, unlike today when parents in their 40's announce they have become grandparents. There should be a minimum age before acquiring this title of distinction.

In his later years, he made his home among his children. He lived with us six months of the year. We were five of his grandchildren—all boys—and I often wondered why he would subject himself to this. Although he was with us for months every year, I only have general memories of him with a few specific isolated images.

He spent time in his room listening to Houston Astros baseball and to boxing. He would often sit on the front porch in his nylon strapped chair enjoying the outdoors, smoking an occasional Camel cigarette, reading the newspaper, and passing his days in grandfatherly thoughts.

Born in 1879 in South Texas, he grew up in an area that consisted mainly of ranches and small communities. Already in his 70's, he was a history book. Unfortunately, I was a non-reader. I could not appreciate his life which had roots in the previous century. In perspective, he was born 34 years after Texas became a state, 14 years after the Civil War ended, and 29 years before the Model T went into production. What was it like growing up in that era, in a place that was once part of

Mexico, at a time when the culture was beginning to transition with Anglo and Mexican influence?

As a child, I did not take time to know my grandfather. I knew nothing of his wife who had died and whom I never had the opportunity to know. My grandmother was just someone who found her spot on the family genealogy chart. We never talked about her, but I am sure he could have related many stories about his wife.

My grandfather lived with us many years, and he was exactly that—my grandfather who lived with us. He passed away at age 92, nearly a century of living history I failed to explore. I really knew nothing about his early life when he grew up as a young boy. To have tapped into the his life would have been fascinating, to hear about life in the 1800's, but I was too busy being a child. I loved him as my grandfather, and perhaps that was more important at the time.

CHAPTER 27

Hot Summer Days

SUMMER WAS ALWAYS HOT, typical of South Texas. They said the temperature was hot enough to fry an egg on the sidewalk; and I tried numerous times, always resulting in a mess—only to find out later it was a figure of speech. They used to say it was so hot, they got evaporated milk from the cows. I never attempted my hand at that. I didn't like powdered milk.

In any case, we knew it was hot; and shorts, t-shirts, and a layer of sweat were our normal attire for summer. As kids, we accepted the heat as part of life. In school, we had learned about the four seasons; but to us, it was book knowledge and material for tests. In South Texas, we had two seasons—hot and hotter.

Our home was not air conditioned, and the two fans we had were shared—usually designated for the kitchen and tv room. On Sundays, my father claimed one for the bedroom. He worked everyday except Sunday, and we felt he deserved it. Opening the windows usually welcomed a small breeze into the rooms, but there was no predictable pattern. Some days were motionless—no sway of the palm fronds, no rustle in the trees, more still than a dead dog with rigor mortis.

At school, there was no air conditioning as well. The heat and the sweat were tolerable, normal for Texas and accepted as part of life. We did not let the heat stop us from a game of kickball or basketball during our free time. However, something was different now entering into middle school. There was an air about us—a stench to be more precise.

As preteens, we carried a collective odor into the classroom which no one ever addressed or acknowledged. No one commented on it; no one pointed fingers. The odor blanketed the room; we were all guilty. It was like the elephant in the room no spoke about except in this case, it was more like the herd had gathered in one place.

I do not know how the girls tolerated us. They never sweated like the boys. We just did not care at the time—at least until we started to notice the girls.

The one fan in each classroom was not adequate. It circulated the heat but it also distributed the odor evenly to all. We learned to make our own fans, a polite way of blowing the odor in the other direction. Our fan-making was basic—creating short alternating folds on a looseleaf sheet of paper. They were effective at any speed, and they lasted as long as the hand could keep oscillating.

The heat did take its toll. At home, we could not mow the yard, especially during peak hours of the afternoon. We could not rake, cut the edges, or trim the bushes. Work was out of the question. This was one area all the brothers had agreed upon.

The heat, however, did not sideline us. It provided a perfect setting for water balloon fights as a fun way of cooling off. My father thought it was a good idea, and he encouraged us to pull out the water hose and soak each other. We took his prompt, surprised that he provoked such a creative suggestion. "And while you're at it," he injected, "you can wash the car and bathe the dog." Our short-sightedness as children did not see that coming.

Today, the days of summer continue to scorch South Texas; but we have discovered alternative ways to cool off. We no longer splash in the yard, attack each other with water balloons, or soak ourselves with the hose. Some things fade with childhood.

However, what my father taught us remains to this day. Some things do not change. I still have to wash the car and bathe the dog.

CHAPTER 28

Embarrassments

THE DAY STARTED LIKE any other workday except I had sported a tie for a scheduled appointment. Arriving early at my desk, I ambled down the hall to the break room for that morning boost of caffeine. I was not the only one arriving early. A young woman with cup in hand also approached; and we exchanged the routine, almost robotic "Good morning."

I had a ten-step advantage, and I initiated a mental race to the coffee pot while trying not to appear deliberate or rude. Too often I had entered the break room to find the pot empty, left by some unscrupulous, inconsiderate caffeine-addicted co-worker who had siphoned the remains of the coffee. I intended on getting to the coffee first. This time I was lucky.

Pouring my coffee, I heard a mumble and a hesitant voice directed toward me. Maybe my race to the break room was not so subtle, and the young woman was about to lash out with unrestrained anger and accusations of selfish intentions on my part. I turned toward her and interrupted to cut off any opportunity for chastisement. It was too early to deal with negativity. Instead, I smiled and politely offered, "May I fill your cup to start this beautiful day?"

She extended her cup to accept my courtesy and again stuttered with hesitation. "Uh, uh, not that I was looking but you have a tear on the, uh, backside of your pants." I reached behind expecting a small rip, a worn section, or a tiny hole. My hand slipped through the mid-seam where I put my fist completely inside, down to the crotch section. The seam had separated—actually ripped—leaving a seven-inch gap. My jaw dropped in disbelief.

When I had looked in the mirror in the morning, my shirt was crisp, my pants ironed, my shoes polished, and my tie in perfect match. Everything about me was right; but I missed the big picture and it became a lesson of humility for me. The young woman spoke nervously but with honesty and respect. I expressed my gratitude because, if she had remained in silence, my day would have had a different outcome. People would have seen a side of me I had not shown before.

I felt guilty in my selfishness; but in this case, being selfish paid off. To serve my needs, I had rushed ahead of her to the break room. I justified my actions, finding consolation the young lady would not have noticed my pants if I had allowed her to go ahead of me.

I retired the pants from my wardrobe. I continued to cross paths with the young lady at work. She never reminded me of the incident—no comments, no looks, not even a smile that would hint of flashbacks. I was not as dismissive. Whenever I caught sight of her, I found my hand inconspicuously reaching behind to check my trousers.

Life hands us embarrassments. They keep us humble; they keep us alert. My embarrassment was minor. Now I can reminisce; now I can laugh. With time, the seriousness of life melts into random episodes of comedy. Being my own audience, I can recall these incidents and still enjoy the re-runs. Sometimes, we need to dismiss our pride and learn to laugh at life's little pranks.

CHAPTER 29

Boring Days

BY MIDSUMMER, time itself took a vacation. Days were endless, and everything moved in slow motion. The initial excitement of a summer break from school had faded into boredom.

"There is nothing to do," cycled in my head as I wandered around the house from room to room, looking aimlessly into the closet, the toy box, and opening drawers. I anticipated a magical genie popping out to entertain me. He never came.

Something in the air depleted the energy from everything. Our dog lay motionless on the front porch, his head cushioned on his paw as he stared with a fixed stupor toward the yard. An errant cat passing through the neighborhood could not rouse the dog's inertia.

No clouds, no breeze. There was silence in the trees, no cackling grackles or flitting sparrows in the leaves. Normally a bed of activity of foraging workers, the ant bed lay abandoned. A lone bumble bee fluttered near the oleander, only to make a quick entrance to his home honed into one of the branches.

Another round through the house, a peek into the toy box, and a check into the closet yielded the same results as before. Boredom abounded in every room but I dared not voice my boredom. My mother always had a list of suggestions to fill the void.

Days like this were infrequent; but the intensity and duration were endless from the perspective of a child. Being bored was a symptom I did not understand at the time, but it seemed rooted on a false notion that I had to be engaged incessantly in some activity.

As an adult, I have gained sensitivity to the subtle movements within me. There is time for action; there is time to be still. It is the yin and yang of life, a balance, a seeking of equilibrium between my external world of constant movement and my internal world of thought and reflection. Much of society is driven by action and constant stimulation while the internal falls to neglect and decay.

My days of boredom as a child remind me to see and practice this balance, to spend time in thoughtful reflection and to be attuned to my spiritual nature. My external world makes more sense and has more purpose when rooted and filtered through my internal core.

We owe it to ourselves to nurture this balance. We owe it to our children to teach this awareness. Boredom is only a symptom seeking to bring equilibrium to ourselves.

CHAPTER 30

Rainy Days

SOME DAYS WERE SO still one could hear the earth gasping for relief from the summer heat. Scattered droplets teased the ground, and the drooping plants were alerted with the promise of rain. Showers had been predicted; and surprisingly true to forecast, they arrived early in the morning—sweeping in with blowing dirt and scattering debris from the dried foliage.

The adults could be heard welcoming the showers, long overdue after weeks of scorching weather. For us kids, however, it signaled a day trapped indoors. Video games and cable television did not exist; and the two local TV stations played re-runs during the summer months.

Being five brothers, we considered options to fill our day;

and if the showers persisted, we could face a week of confinement. Chess and Scrabble were fun in the beginning, but these games demanded higher level thinking. Being brother four and lower on the cognitive totem pole, I was usually on the losing end; and soon, the fun of playing lost its appeal.

On a more level playing field, knowing I had a chance, we engaged in marathon Monopoly—games which lasted for hours, sometimes days. On other days, we would alternate with card games by combining three decks and playing Battle. This simple high-card playoff would take us late into the night and often into subsequent days. We never tired of these repetitive games, driven by determination of beating the other.

Battle escalated into War, a home-made version of opposing armies. Recruitment for the armies came from our father's auto parts store. Saturday was the day we helped our dad by sweeping the floors, cleaning the windows, arranging merchandise, and filling the Coke machine. The Coke machine was the source of recruitment as we emptied the bottle caps from the week's sales. The bottle caps served as the armies, and we divided them evenly among the players.

Coke and Dr. Pepper were the most common caps, and they became the general frontline soldiers to fill the ranks. The less common caps were designated to be officers—Grapette, Nehi Orange, and Royal Crown Cola. Special forces were formed from the Lone Star, Schlitz, and Pabst Blue Ribbon beer caps which were collected from the family barbecues.

Each player had his strategy. The armies of 100 quickly dwindled, as they were killed in action by attacking and shooting marbles at each other. Eventually, one army would be victorious, usually one of the beer brigades, Schlitz being my favorite.

Nature always took its turn, and sunny days again became the norm. Like caterpillars in a cocoon, we ventured out of our confinement to return to our routines of cruising the neighborhoods on our bikes, joining a football game at the corner lot, or catching up with friends who like us had been bored for days.

Childhood energy was not intended to be cooped up too long. In children's time, one day of confinement was excessive. From our parents' perspective as well, one day of being cooped up was *beyond* excessive with having five children confined indoors.

Our parents had found relief with the summer rains. They found greater relief with the return of the sun.

CHAPTER 31

Surviving Life

TRADITIONALLY, TWENTY-ONE marks the age of passage into adulthood. For me, it marked the official end of my childhood. I finally had crossed the finish line in the Indy 500 of growing up; and now adulthood was the trophy for having survived all the treacherous laps as a kid.

Being active, being a child, and being a boy were ingredients for injuries, bumps, bruises, and every description that falls into the category of accidents. "We were just playing, it was an accident, I didn't mean to, it was his fault, he started it, and it just happened" all were common commentaries in our family of five brothers. I was not immune from my share of accidents; and I often wondered how I survived the years.

"Come on," my brother prodded me, "Get on." Rocket to the Moon was an impromptu game we played in the yard. The name clearly described how to play. My brother lay on his back with his bent legs facing upward to provide a seat and launching pad for me. I sat on the soles of his feet, found my balance, and waited for the blast off.

"Three, two, one" and my brother projected me into the air. I had previous flight experience, but I was not prepared to be put into orbit. The landing was rough as I cushioned the fall with my outstretched arm. I avoided a break, but I remained in a sling for a week with a sprain.

I experienced only one broken bone as a child. The neighborhood band of boys had gathered for a baseball game at the local park. We brought what we had and shared—a few bats and gloves, old cushions for bases, and a baseball.

One of the boys surprised us with a new baseball he had received for his birthday. We were able to retire "old faithful," the worn grassed-stained ball which had a two-inch rip on the seams. I was playing the distance, left field; and I waited for the batter to take position. We had been short one glove, and I shared mine with my younger brother in right field. The batter shifted his body, grasped the bat, and glanced briefly my way. I crouched and prepared.

Wham! The solid hit crossed the infield in the air. The ball bounced and headed in my direction. I ran towards the ball, timing the projectile so I could scoop it up on the first bounce. In slight miscalculation, the ball jammed my little finger. The pain was immediate, and the 45-degree angle of my finger suggested that something was out of the ordinary.

I signaled a time-out and trotted to the infield to show the others. They saw it and laughed. They knew I was double-jointed, and they accused me of playing a joke. Falsely charged and pulsating in pain, I walked home while the others continued the game.

My mother did not look surprised. It was another day in the life of a mother of five boys. A visit to the doctor confirmed a break, and my hand was put into a cast. My brothers still did not believe me. I had the evidence, and I came home and showed them the finger.

Injuries always happened in a flash, unforeseen and never in a moment of preparation. In soccer, there was always an inexperienced player who would miss the ball and land a misguided—or perhaps intentional—kick into the groin of the opponent. Sometimes, I was the inexperienced player; sometimes I was the opponent. Every male can recount being kicked in the crotch. It was a rite of passage.

In basketball, it was the jammed fingers and sprained ankles. In track, it was the pole vaulter who kicked the crossbar to my face, leaving me with a bruised eye. But not all accidents were sports related.

An angry brother chased me into the yard trying to hit me with a broom. I outran him as I jumped into the neighbor's yard. He hurled the broom which hit the fence; and the broom flipped while continuing toward his target. The wooden knob slammed my forehead, leaving a bump—no, a one inch protrusion—for four days.

I cannot recount all the incidents—too many to retrieve from memory. I received a scar next to the eye, a torn gum line, a twisted tooth, a wound to the back of the head, crushed fingers in the car door, a baseball to the face, and multiple black eyes from horseplay and other childhood activities.

Childhood was like an obstacle course. I had been able to complete it but not without some of the collisions and bruising that went with it. Viewed in isolation, I was the poster child for accidents; but all the neighborhood kids—at least the boys—related similar experiences. With five boys in the family, our parents lived with a perpetual question, "What now?" as life presented them with many surprises as we grew up.

Despite our history, our parents never discouraged nor forbade us from engaging in the rough sports or the games of childhood. They always cushioned their permission with "be careful" for whatever that was worth, but we listened and did our best. We all made it to the finish line of childhood.

CHAPTER 32

The Church Experience

"HERE IS THE KEY to the church," the pastor said as he handed over two keys. "The other one is to the rectory in case you change your mind." I took the keys to his house as a courtesy but happier the pastor was open to my idea of spending the night in the church.

It was summer of my 10th grade year and I was experiencing a spiritual awakening. Years of Catholic education had taught me the heroism of Christians—both adults and children—who had given their lives to God. Early Christians were imprisoned, tortured, and torn apart by lions as entertainment for the crowds. Stories of saints provided descriptions of death by stoning, crucifixion, and beheading. Others were clubbed, grilled alive, or crushed to death.

The stories were gruesome but inspiring, but I thought a non-violent approach was more my style. Martyrdom could wait. My immediate plan was to spend an all-night vigil in a sacred setting.

At 10:00 p.m., I slipped through the sacristy door and entered the sanctuary. I knelt on the step near the altar as I was drawn to silence, and I easily entered into prayer and meditative images. An overwhelming sense of peace settled, and a whispering voice within captured the moment. "I could stay forever."

Forever lasted eight minutes. A loud cracking sound erupted from the pew in the back. "What was that?" I thought as my face reacted with startle and fear. "Anyone there?" I called out to the whole church. There was no answer, and a second popping followed from the other side. I remained in the sanctuary, shaking nervously as I scanned the church.

No lights were on, only candles flickering in one of the devotional stations in the back, causing shadows to dance on the walls. More images could be seen through the stained-glass windows. They resembled people trying to get in as the figures swayed from side to side.

The Church was locked, so no one else was inside—unless, of course, they had been hiding in the choir loft. I called out one more time and then made a slow visual review of all the benches, row by row. I creeped down the middle aisle, expecting nothing but anticipating the unimaginable. Fear escalates quickly when dealing with the unknown.

Prayer came easily but not in the peaceful fashion as I had started. I prayed the Lord's Prayer but I stuck on the last line, "deliver us from evil." "Were these only shadows," I wondered, "or were they spirits at work?"

More creaking and cracking erupted, but now the tension of my body began to relax. Rational thought began to return as I could see the creaking was a natural reaction of the wooden benches and the summer humidity. No spirits at play. My mind accepted the rational, but my heart's pumping was not yet in sync with my thoughts. I consigned myself to return to prayerful reflection.

The pews continued to creak, and the shadows continued their tease on my imagination. They were no longer a threat, but they were a constant distraction. At 2:00 a.m., I recalled the words of the pastor—"the second key, in case you change your mind." He must have known something when he had offered it.

I slithered into the residence and found comfort in the guest room. I knew God could speak in dreams, and I gave Him the opportunity as I slipped into bed. My thoughts drifted back to the lives of the saints. They were courageous in facing dangers and threats because of their convictions; and I succumbed to the perceived threats of shadows and noises.

I did not abandon my desire to become a saint, and I trusted God would eventually lead me there; but I conceded my destiny would be the patron of wimps and cowards. The beauty of the Church is that there is a place for everyone, and I was willing to accept this lowly place with great humility.

CHAPTER 33

The Horned Toad

TOADS, LIZARDS, AND AN occasional garden snake caught our attention as children playing in the backyard. We would prod the toad with a broken branch from the hackberry tree just to see the creature hop a few steps. They always looked lethargic, sitting on their rears, with large bulging eyes staring off into nowhere, and having no place to go except where they were.

Toads never seemed bothered, and we bored quickly with their inattention to us. Lizards on the other hand were fast. They would stop in their tracks, stare at us momentarily; and if we made any movement toward them, they would dart and zig-zag to escape. Their evolutionary history must have had a lot of experience with kids. They instinctively fled from us without a second thought.

Among all the reptiles, insects, and creepy-crawlers in the neighborhood, horned toads gained special respect from us. Kids called them by different names—horned frogs, horned lizards, or horny toads, the last being the most common. Their stature was prehistoric—stout, wide-bodied with short legs and tail, grayish brown in color, covered in scales with thorn-like spines from front to back. They resembled a miniature dinosaur, ferocious in appearance but with a gentle nature.

Whenever we caught sight of the horny toad, we aimed to capture it. They had speed but not comparable to the lizards; and they could be cornered, especially if surrounded by three kids. When threatened, the horned creature was capable of flattening his body to blend in with the dirt or bloat to twice his size—a phenomenon we witnessed several times.

Once captured, the horny toad lay in full compliance. He did not struggle; he did not bite. We had heard he could spit blood at his enemies through his eyes, something we never witnessed; but we did not want to find out the hard way.

Massaging his belly would put him to sleep—or perhaps he was just pretending, waiting for us to relax our guard in a planned attempt to escape. He never made a lunge so we interpreted it to mean that he found comfort in being stroked.

With his horned head, rough scales, and spiny body, I imagine he did not do much cuddling with his mate or share affection with his peers. The massage may have been a treat for him.

We always released the horny creatures back into their natural domain, and they would quickly disappear into the undergrowth. We saw horned toads regularly in the yard, in the alley, or in the city parks. Eventually, they became scarce. It was not just in the neighborhood as they made it on the list of threatened species in Texas. With its popularity and unique stature, the Texas Horned Lizard was designated the official reptile of the state.

The decline of the species was attributed to the loss of habitat and his food source of red ants. I did not know this information as a child, and I had attributed the scarcity to the mischievous kids in the neighborhood.

It is a remarkable commentary how a reptile can gain the fascination and affection of not only a few curious children, but also to see how it captured the attention of the entire state to elevate it as the official reptile.

The horned toad resembled a creature from the age of dinosaurs, and unfortunately it is heading in the same direction of extinction.

CHAPTER 34

Apple Pie

IT WAS ALL ABOUT THE PIE, the moment in life when I felt like an adult. There was a psychological breakthrough, a new mindset. It was a distinct moment. I was already handling the rent, utilities, car, gas, and groceries; but these were the expected responsibilities of growing up.

A family of five boys meant everything was shared. I was son number four, so hand-me-downs filled my wardrobe. Parents were creative in preparing dishes that would stretch to feed the whole family. Rice, beans, *fideo,* and tortillas were the staples. These were inexpensive, and they could be prepared in large batches. A pot of beans was always on the stove, and tortillas could be made easily.

Rice and fideo took on many variations, enhanced with cuts of meat, chicken, or vegetables. They were magically converted to our favorite dishes of *arroz con pollo, arroz con puerco, or calabaza con pollo.* They were not always the best cuts of meat, but they provided flavor. As children, taste was always more important than health. Our parents fed us what they could afford. As children, we never complained about being hungry.

As children, dessert seldom made it to the table, except on holidays and celebrations. Now as a young adult and living on my own, the image of apple pie flashed in my head and played on my emotional cravings. I sat in my apartment and debated whether to concede to my impulses—a debate easily won. My cravings drove me with compulsion to the grocery store.

The apple pies on the shelves did not meet the mouth-drooling mental images I had entertained earlier; but I was determined not to leave empty-handed. I selected one with a thick crust, browned to perfection with sprinkles of cinnamon. It turned out to be mainly dough, slightly dry but with a few juicy slices that appeared to be apples. Compared to others, the pie looked scrumptious, with my imagination filling in what was missing. I needed no basket; I ran to the checkout.

At home, I sat at the table with the apple pie staring back at me, seducing me with its aroma of apples and cinnamon. I had seen many pies in my life but this was an experience like no other. I had the whole pie to myself, and I could eat it all. I did not have to share. The dessert did not have to stretch to all my siblings and parents. This was *my* pie, and I was ready to indulge.

My first bite was intense as I held a small chunk of apple on

my tongue, savoring the interplay of flavors of the crust and the sweetness of the juices. This called for an encore as I drew a second slice from the pie. Soon after, a third. I was experiencing a taste of heaven. Twenty minutes passed and I still had half a pie.

My palate at this point had become saturated, my eyes however still feeling undernourished. Fixated on this opportunity, I continued my indulgence. "This was my pie, and I could eat it all" became my mantra. The next bite, however, was repulsive. I coughed it up and spewed it on the floor. I threw the rest away, and I did not eat apple pie for months. I did not eat *any* pie for months.

The apple pie was a moment when I asserted my independence. I was not under the rule of family. I could make decisions. I could pursue my interests. As I look back, I recognized how silly—actually stupid—the incident was. I was relieved no one was around to witness my gluttony. However, it was an important step in understanding what it meant to be an adult. It was all about the pie.

CHAPTER 35

The Mean Streak

I WAS INCONSIDERATE. I was 8-years old, so perhaps mischievous is more accurate.

I went to the front yard to bring my bike closer to the house. We did not use locks in those days; and leaving the bike unwatched in the front a few hours was the norm. We did not worry about theft, but we did take care to bring it in by the evening.

As I stood the bike up, I noticed a reflection coming through the blades of grass. "Hmm, a hair band," I exclaimed. Although it fit my head snuggly, I knew it was not mine. Yes, even as an 8-year old, I felt compelled to try it on—this being the mischievous and the boy in me. I then turned to make sure no one was watching when my judgment caught up with my actions and I realized how foolish I must have looked. Only our dog caught eye of me, and he did not even crack a smile.

We were five boys in the family, so I correctly assumed the hair band belonged to none of us—yes, assumed. Being homophobic or having gender stereotypes were not questions of the day. We were just practical. We all had short hair, and no one had need of a hair band.

Our neighbors had two girls, so I had surmised the hair band belonged to one of them. They were both younger and they were friends; so I began to march the band over to their house. My good intentions began to dissolve by my fifth step. I spotted a pile of dog dung in the yard which I could have bypassed easily.

I stopped in silence, in awe at the hefty pile that stood before me. It had to have been a Great Dane or German Shepherd or some very constipated poodle. How quickly thoughts churn and feed the imagination. Two angels found position on my shoulders, each whispering in my ear. The one on the left prodded me, "Do it, do it." The voice spoke with authority. The one on the right jumped in with louder voice, "Do it NOW!"

The angels were unlike the cartoons with opposing views. They conspired with one voice, and my mind complied with no argument.

I scooped the fresh poop with the hair band, carried it to the neighbors, and dropped it in their front yard. I ran back to get my bike, scurried to the backyard, and went inside the house.

I did not see the hair band in the yard the next morning. I never found out if it belonged to one of the girls. I never inquired with them if anyone had discovered anything unusual. I never saw either girl wearing it over the next month.

The incident happened, and no reference to it was ever made by anyone. However, it remained clear in my mind; I knew what had happened. To this date, I often wondered what prompted me to extend this un-neighborly gesture.

I was 8-years-old, a boy, and inconsiderate, perhaps mischievous and playful being more accurate. No, I was mean.

CHAPTER 36

Young Businessmen

PERHAPS IT WAS THE MONEY; perhaps it was the fun. Perhaps it was just being children seeking ways to fill the days with adventure. We received a small allowance but we sought ways to supplement our income. Nobody wanted to sell watermelons. They were too bulky, and they were not alway in season. Cupcakes were too much trouble, and we were too young to sell cold beer on a hot summer day. We were still in elementary.

We lived on our bikes, always trekking across town to a friend's house, doing our paper route, or taking a quick trip to the grocery store for bread or milk. We often found soft drink bottles on the roads or thrown into bushes. These were refundable, only worth a few cents, but a find of four would buy a cold Coke after finishing the paper route on a scorching day.

We tried the Kool-Aid stands in the front yard, but these never proved profitable. We would extend credit to neighborhood kids and we would drink the rest of the proceeds. We kept busy but we made no money.

We found it more profitable to use the Kool-Aid to make home-made Pixie Stix. We blended the raw Kool-Aid with a batch of sugar, filled straws, and sealed the two ends with candle wax. At school, we fetched a penny a piece; and the demand always exceeded the supply.

We expanded our inventory to include cinnamon sticks, made overnight by soaking toothpicks in cinnamon oil available over-the-counter at the pharmacy. Surprisingly, the sisters at school never prohibited our sales nor even cautioned us that we might poke someone's eye out if not careful. They allowed us to be entrepeneurs in our simple ways.

The sisters never offered to buy our Pixie Stix or our cinnamon toothpicks. I imagine they had their own stash of goodies under their hefty robes. I always imagined a hidden flask with church wine tucked behind their rosary beads. The sisters loved their rosaries. Our sales remained steady for the few weeks we were in business, and we stuffed our few pennies in profits into our piggy banks.

We heard the old axiom, "A penny saved is a penny earned." I guess we took it too literally. Our business did make cents, and that was on the best of days; but it made no sense to continue for the meager income. We dropped our business ventures and focused on more important things. I am not sure what those were as a child, perhaps praying for world peace or how we could feed the starving children of China. Our success with that seemed comparable to our business dealings.

The calls to adventure, creativity, and imagination were plentiful as children. We always had plans in the making, activities on the drawing board, and projects to implement. The results were not impressive but the experiences were enriching. They say "A profit is never accepted in his own land" and we proved that to be true.

CHAPTER 37

God's Team

WE HUDDLED FOR PRAYER. The game was about to start, and we wanted to invoke the Head Coach in the heavens to guide our team to victory. We were a Catholic school, and prayer was part of our daily routine. We felt God would give us an edge when playing other teams during football season.

Our theory—and unfounded hope—quickly dissipated. We were reminded we were a church league, and all our opponents were also Catholic schools in the region. "God can't take sides," we were told, but I believed he had his favorites. This year, I knew it was not our team.

I was in 8th grade and tryouts were announced. We were a small school, and everyone who showed up was given a position. I had hoped to become a receiver, but I was designated as quarterback. That was the first premonition of a bad year. I was shorter than five feet, and I weighed less than 100 pounds. I sensed a year of desperation for our team.

The first play of our season, I scurried back with the ball and threw a long pass down field, and the receiver ran in for a touchdown. The cheers erupted but quickly fizzled when the referee threw the yellow flag. The score was nullified, and we failed to score again. We lost the game, and the season went down from there.

By the third game, we set our eyes on victory. We were facing a tough team, and we had heard our opponents planned on bringing former students who were now in high school. Not to be outdone, our team contacted former students as well. They showed up on game day and suited up for play.

We won the game, but it did not matter. The league administrator—who also was our pastor—suspended our team for the rest of the season for cheating. There was little grumbling. The team accepted the consequences.

Some questions remained open. Who initiated the rumor of the opponent's plan to put in illegal players? How did *our* coach accept the rumors and allow us to put in illegal players?

On the down side, our team forfeited the rest of the games. On the positive side, our short season limited us to only two losses. Yes, we cheated on our third game, but we won. It would have been worse to have cheated and lost.

Two Catholic teams prayed for victory that day. In his way, God heard the prayers of both. We won the game, and the other team took the victory. It was a win-win situation, and God had the last laugh.

CHAPTER 38

Monster Under the Bed

IT WAS THERE AGAIN. I was sure. I was five years old. I lay in bed fearful of the dark, afraid of the monster under the bed. It was waiting for me as it always did at night. I couldn't turn, and I had to be careful my arm did not slip over the edge toward the floor. I do not know why I felt safe on the bed as if the monster could not grab me there. Life is not always rational at that age.

I do not recall how old I was when the monster starting coming to my room. How it got there or why it chose to be there was never questioned.

Friends shared the same fear. It was always at night when the lights were off. Some friends said they slept with the light on; others still slept with their parents. I was too embarrassed to do either—or at least admit to it.

Parents always advised us not to worry—easy for them as the monsters preferred being in the children's room. We had never seen the monster, but we had seen shadows move about the room. Perhaps there was more than one monster. We did not know, but we sensed a silent and mysterious presence

This was at the time communities started putting pictures of missing children on milk cartons; and we believed there was a connection. We never heard of children we knew to be lost; but we never heard of any children being found. Our fears were justified.

With daylight coming, I would check under my bed—not once, not twice, but repeatedly *to be sure*—and I never saw anything except for an occasional dirty sock that had been missing for months. Something about the night that always returned the fear.

Was there really a monster under my bed? Did he snatch children from their homes? As I grew older, I chuckled at the idea of a monster. "Childhood fantasy," I concluded.

I remember, however, the feeling of that childhood fear. It was intense. It was real. It was petrifying. I realized later the feeling never went away completely. I remembered it as an adolescent, again as a teen, and then into adult life.

"That feeling," I thought was the monster I had never seen. The monster was never under my bed. It was the monster within— the fears I encountered through life, only with different faces.

Now I have learned to sleep in peace. However, I still look under the bed in daylight. I see no monsters; I harbor no fears. Occasionally, I receive small consolation in finding the lost sock which had evaded its pair for months.

CHAPTER 39

Dogs

ALL FIVE BOYS IN the family had distinct personalities; but we all shared in a common trait, a love for pets. Attention to the pets diverted many fights and rumbles we would have had as brothers. Our parents in their quiet wisdom must have known this; and they allowed us to bring a zoo full of animals into the household.

Over the years, we became a host family to rabbits, pigeons, parakeets, fish, chameleons, rats, hamsters, snakes, guinea pigs, and generations of cats and dogs. Dogs dominated the list, and most were mutts—usually a mixture of whatever roamed the neighborhood.

Leash laws were non-existent; and there was never a shortage of dogs in the streets. Like the residents, the dogs had their personalities. As bike riders, it was critical we learn the personalities of the dogs in the different sections of town.

We did not know dogs by breed but by behavior and by neighborhood. Most dogs remained oblivious to our passing. Other dogs barked spontaneously when they saw us. The bark was their way of letting us know we were in their territory, and they were letting us pass without incident. The third type of dog was most vicious. They were quiet and conniving. They waited for small children on their bikes and attacked in stealth mode.

We knew what to do. We pumped the pedals with full strength, getting up to optimum speed, and we would race through the neighborhood. If the dog did not emerge, we figured he had captured his prey for the day, some new kid in the neighborhood who did not know the rules of riding.

Most times the dog was ready and began the chase. We were always vigilant, aware that even a small dog could leave an

impression on the tender flesh of a child. If we could make it to the end of the block, we would be safe as the dog relented and returned to his station awaiting another child.

It was not easy. Even at top speed, the dog kept pace, barking viciously while showing his fangs and snipping at our ankles. We learned to pedal with one foot while we kicked at the dog's face in desperate defense. Somehow the experienced riders always made it.

All the boys in the neighborhood had their stories. One would brag with straight face, "I made it through the block on 9th street, with 20 dogs chasing after me." A second boy would counter, "The dog that chased me was bigger than my bike, but I gave it one good kick in the snout to show him who's boss."

Everyone had been snipped, bitten, or had their jeans ripped while cycling through neighborhoods. The experiences made great stories, and they set the stage for bragging rights. I always wondered if the dogs did the same—recounting the chases and embellishing their stories among themselves. I am sure that our stories would not match with theirs. No doubt, their stories would be more credible.

Today's dogs bring shame to their breed. They are pampered to an extreme. They are bathed, blow-dried, trimmed, and brushed. They have their nails manicured, their teeth brushed, and dressed in cute outfits from their seasonal wardrobe. They have a trunk full of favorite toys, treats for afternoon snacks, and a cushy pillow and blanket to relieve them from the stresses of the day. They garnish more attention from the family than we received as kids.

With today's leash laws, dogs do not roam as before. They have surrendered the rule of their neighborhoods. They have given up their pursuit of children trespassing into their territory. As a consequence, children ride *leisurely* through the streets without incident not knowing the history of their neighborhood —the attacks, the defenses, and the blood shed by their ancestors. Today's children do not understand the true meaning of the dog days of summer. Above all, they have lost the exhilaration of the chase.

Dogs have a saying that "man is dog's best friend" and humans have lived up to this reputation.

CHAPTER 40

Not To Be Outdone

WE MADE THE FINAL count, "88, 89, 90." The day was boring, and my friend and I were seeking creative ways to fill the day. We had 90 pieces of gum, not just any gum but Double-Bubble. They were not the slender sticks one politely slipped into the mouth for refreshment. Double-Bubble came as chunks of pink chewing gum. Two or three in the mouth provided ammunition for blowing serious bubbles.

Dividing the load, the challenge was made. "Let's see who can put the most into our mouths." The gum was hard on the bite and tough on the jaws; but that did not prevent the duel. Competition ignited determination, "21, 22, 23" and room for more as each continued to cram pieces into the mouth. Piercing stares elevated the challenge to a higher level; the persistent drool reduced it to the crude contest that it was.

Double-Bubble was made for boys. No girl could maintain her feminine poise trying to handle the salivary excretions. Boys were slobs, and we lived up to the image.

My friend reached his goal first, having stuffed 45 pieces of gum into his mouth. Not to be outdone, I managed to tie four minutes later by matching his accomplishment. We laughed at our foolishness, gazing at each other's chipmunk faces—our stuffed cheeks still wet and sticky.

"Hey, it's not over," he quickly challenged. "Give me your gum," he insisted. I complied and handed him the wad from my mouth. He grasped the slithery mass, squeezed hard to eject the encapsulated saliva, and slowly slipped small pieces into his mouth. He did it, all 90 pieces, stuffed inside his cheeks. More drool began to flow.

He was the winner. "But wait," I retorted. "It's only fair for me to have a chance at accomplishing the same." Our contest ended in a tie.

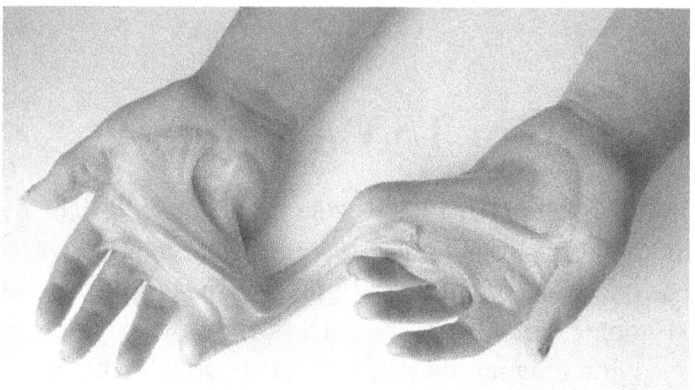

Decades later, I reminisced on this incident and asked how we ventured to this duel. We accomplished nothing. We set no records for Guinness. We did not make it into an annual event nor challenge others to this feat. The incident faded into history.

At the time, we were young and we were friends. We shared a moment of boredom and transformed it into a memorable incident. We played, we laughed, and our segment of history was shared with each other. Since then, we have both moved on.

The incident was foolish and gross; but no harm was done. Yes, our pride was at stake; but worse has been done in the name of pride. Harmless foolishness is healthy for life. Those who have ventured into this territory can relate. The gross part can be dismissed.

CHAPTER 41

Prejudice

AS A CHILD, I DO NOT recall experiencing any prejudice. Perhaps I was too naive to recognize it. Being Hispanic, I had heard terms "greaser" and "wetback," both of which were not used as flattery. However, I never had these directed toward me or my friends. We never used them in conversation.

Catholic school provided a positive environment, and even the use of cuss words was not tolerated. The worst I recall was use of the "s-word" and this did not stand for saint."

As children, we were naive about many things. We even used terminology we did not know was racist or derogatory. Living on the border, we crossed the Rio Grande to go to the Mexican market. Everyone knew how it worked. The first price that was offered would always be high. We took that as a starting point and tried to "Jew them down" as part of the bargaining routine. We used the term as a functional word. I did not even know any Jews; and I certainly did not use the term with derogatory intent.

In those days, most of the neighborhood boys had slingshots. We made our own, using the instructions from oral traditions and experience. A reliable slingshot depended on the skills and practice of the elders in the neighborhood.

We found a strong y-shaped branch from the Hackberry tree and whittled it down to fit one's grasp. We rummaged through our bike's old tire tubes, cut rubber strips to make stretch bands and attached them to the handle. The Chinaberry tree provided an endless supply of marble-sized balls for our ammunition.

We were warriors with our weapons. Lizards, cicadas, and any other unsuspecting creatures were not safe when the neighborhood boys went on patrol. We cherished our slingshots, and took pride in our craftsmanship.

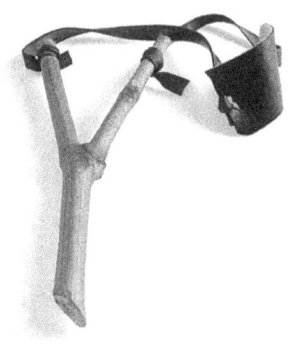

However, we often called them by their other name—"the N... shooter. This was a name we knew, a name that was common, and a name used as learned vocabulary. In a similar way, we often played Fox Across the River, otherwise known as "N..... Across the Cornfield." No one ever corrected us as children or commented on any of these terms as being a racial slur to the black race. They were the vocabulary of the neighborhood. I do not know the origins of these derogatory terms we used. We were naive and culturally insulated.

We used these terms naturally, no different than referencing a BB gun or a fly swatter or playing Hide-n-Seek. Somewhere in time, we grew up; and playing these games and using the slingshot faded into childhood history. Not until adulthood did we reminisce and realize how derogatory those terms were. Not until adulthood did we realize how naive we were.

CHAPTER 42

The Fire

THE VOICE DID NOT sound familiar, but the male caller identified as an anonymous neighbor. "Is your roof fireproof?" he asked in a calm voice.

I responded with hesitation, preparing for the punchline. I had prank calls before like the one in which I was asked if my refrigerator was running. I checked and went back to the phone to say that it was. The jokester quickly interjected, "Well, go after it," and he hung up while bellowing with laughter.

I did not want to fall victim again, but I could think of no punchline or any clever response. "I guess the roof is fireproof. Why do you ask?" I waited for an eruption of laughter as I could feel I was being played for a fool. "Well," he reported in the same calm voice, "your roof is on fire."

It was the 4th of July, and fireworks could be heard in the neighborhood. I took the caller's message seriously and checked the roof. The anonymous caller was telling the truth. A small flame was spotted, already spreading across several dry wooden shingles.

My brother quickly exited the house, and we both went into firemen's mode. We had seen rescue movies on television; and without hesitation, we grabbed the water hose. Fortunately, we were able to extinguish the flame before it got out of hand.

Little damage was done, and the firemen checked to ensure all embers were extinguished. A bottle rocket from the neighborhood had found its target on our roof. Perhaps it was the neighbor who was calling; perhaps that is the reason he remained anonymous.

The excitement was short-lived, but it could have erupted into a major incident. I was grateful for the neighbor's call, but I remained suspicious. I still wonder why he asked if our roof was fireproof. What if I had answered yes? That was a strange question; but we also had some strange neighbors.

CHAPTER 43

The Paperboy

IN ELEMENTARY SCHOOL, all five brothers served as paperboys—a term used at that time. I do not think any girls delivered the paper—not that they were not capable, but it just seemed to be a guy-thing. No one ever heard of a papergirl.

Among the brothers, the route was passed on, much like hand-me-down clothing. It did not pay much, but we learned the responsibilities and commitment to the job.

As a perk, we enjoyed shuffling through the change we received looking for old coins for our hobby. We thrilled in finding a Buffalo nickel, a Liberty quarter, an Indian Head penny, or a steel 1943 cent. Occasionally, we found an old fifty-cent piece or a silver dime. These were treasures for us as children.

We became familiar with all our customers, and we gave them personalized service. One preferred the paper placed under the welcome mat, another stuck in the screen door, and another under a large rock on the front porch. Each customer had a preference, and we aimed to please. This is unlike today's delivery which makes each morning like an Easter egg hunt, trying to find the paper hidden in the grass, in the bushes, or sometimes stuck in the tree.

Many customers showed their gratitude with a small Christmas gift—a box of candy canes, the Christmas edition of Life Savers with ten different flavors, or a two-dollar bill which was a novelty at the time.

Among all the customers, one stands out. He had not paid his bill in over three months, despite repeated efforts to collect. I would knock on his door, wait a minute, and repeat the routine two more times. Thursday was collection day, but I tried any day with the hope of catching him.

The front door was usually open, and I could peer in through the outer screen. His living room was in full view. There was no sign of human activity—no music playing, no television, no family or visitors in the room; but I could see his figure, motionless and mute, behind the curtains. No luck today. I would come back and try again, optimistic my efforts would pay off. I continued to deliver believing he would pay some day. That day never came, and I had to absorb the loss.

By now, the old man surely has passed; and ironically, his picture was probably in the obituary section of the paper for which he had refused to pay. I wondered if it mentioned his hiding antics in the obituary narrative. In the dark shadows of my mind, I wrote my own version of his obituary:

"Jack was reported missing for three days before his body was found in his house behind the curtains. He leaves behind three children and an unpaid bill to the paperboy who had to pay out of his own pocket. In lieu of flowers, donations can be sent to this gullible and hopeful child who brought the newspaper faithfully every day. Jack will be missed, just as the paperboy missed him every time he tried to collect."

I recall school days when I could not remember important facts and formulas, but to this day—decades later— I remember the man behind the curtains. I recall his name. I can visualize the house, the screen door, the drapes, and the obscure figure behind them. I recall my thoughts when he would not answer the door. I remember my feelings of disappointment when I walked away from his house.

Being a paperboy was a learning experience in our lives. It provided a small cash flow, but it also thrust us into the demands of the real world. We had to show up—rain or shine, cold or heat. We rode our bikes or walked the entire route, carrying the load of papers over our shoulders in a bag provided by the press. Sunday papers tripled the weight and the bulk. Perhaps this is why girls were not recruited for the job. We never complained about the demands. We never complained about the pay. We just did our job.

None of our peers at school had a paper route, and that made us feel special with our adult-like responsibilities. The experience was irreplaceable, and I would not change anything about it—except of course, the man behind the curtains.

Someday, I too will pass; and hopefully I will be welcomed into heaven where the curtains will be drawn and I can meet this man face-to-face. I would love to hear from him, but I approach with hesitation. He avoided me in life; but now in heaven, he could literally avoid me forever. I will take the chance to bring closure to our unfortunate exchange in life, even if it takes me an eternity.

CHAPTER 44

Random Acts of Nothingness

I DO NOT KNOW HOW the game started—in fact, it did not deserve to be called a game. Technically, there was a winner; but there were no rules or purpose. I guess we did it because we were bored, but being bored and doing nothing made more sense than engaging in this futile activity.

What prompted us to engage in this activity leaves me clueless. This was not a one-time event. I blame it on my brothers because I know I did not come up with the idea.

The count began as cars passed. We would sit on the street corner—in the neighborhood or at a busy intersection—-and pull out our pocket notepads with our favorite ballpoint pen. Not checking the make of car, not noting the state on the license plate, not seeing how many people were inside the car, we would merely write the license plate number on our notepad. This would continue for an hour, two hours, and at times we would continue this practice through the day.

Coming to the dinner table in the evening, we would compare. "How many plates did you get today? There was no prize. There were no congratulatory remarks. We just did it as we were fascinated at making all those entries, and we were determined to beat the other in this game.

At times, we would notice that we made the same entry on our pad. This implied the car had passed earlier in the day.

The driver apparently had gone about his errands, perhaps meeting someone for lunch, watching a movie, stopping for an afternoon coffee, and was now on the way home. I wondered if he had as much fun with his day as I did while I sat on the curb checking license plates.

I never understood why I engaged in this game; but as an eight year-old, I did it a number of times. I must have had fun.

Recently, I observed a group of young teenage girls giggling and acting silly at the mall. One would blurt out a word, another would burp, and the third would point at each other's faces. Each time, the group would burst out laughing as the mindless exchange continued.

No one really said anything, and no one really did anything; but all three lived in a bubble of laughter and nonsense of the moment. I saw no humor in it. I understood nothing of their gestures or grunts; and I concluded I had to be in *their* moment to fully comprehend.

Checking license plates must have been one of those moments in my childhood bubble.

CHAPTER 45

The Mexican Side

THIS WAS TEXAS but every border community had "the Mexican part of town." This was usually south of the railroad tracks. My father had a small business selling auto parts in this section—before the big box stores and the national chains had come into town.

Spanish was the dominant language. First time visitors from northern states always went through culture shock. People were different in deep South Texas. Customs were different, and many of the native population did not speak any English.

The Winter Texans—or Snow Birds as they were called—did not realize they were a few miles from the Mexican border and that this part of the country had a longer history of being part of Mexico than it had with the United States.

Many of the winter visitors adapted quickly, especially when they discovered cheap margaritas, bargain dental care, and inexpensive medications across the Rio Grande.

My father's business survived through the years. In today's business environment, it would have been smothered by the big stores. At that time, however, all the stores in the Mexican part of town were owned by families and not by corporations or the big chains. My father's shop was next to a cafe, specializing in surprisingly—Mexican food. It was a casual place where the one mopping the floor would break to serve the order at the tables. Hair nets and gloves were non-existent. This was before employees had to be reminded "to wash their hands" before leaving the restroom.

Three more Mexican restaurants down the street gave people options. They were simple places meant to serve the working people—good meals, affordable, with a home-cooked style.

Each person had his favorite. People went for the food, not an exquisite ambience. The entrance for one was behind a taxi stand near the alley. The door was accessed by ascending two steps, turning sharply to the right, and then descending another three steps to enter the dining area. Four long wooden tables lined the room, and customers found empty seats to join strangers or friends who were already there. The room was small, the stoves were on, and there was no air conditioning. The atmosphere was accommodating and people squeezed in without complaint to eat a savory meal.

The cook stood behind the counter with food on the back burners, offering a choice of three selections for the day. In the adjoining room was the *tortilleria* where ladies in sweltering heat provided an endless supply of hand-made tortillas. They ensured no table was without a fresh stack. No one complained about the heat. This was South Texas. It was a way of life; and the fresh food and tortillas made it tolerable.

Other businesses lined the street—hair stylists, clothing stores, several finance businesses, bakeries specializing in *pan dulce* or Mexican sweet bread and pastries, two theaters showing the latest Mexican films, and a St. Vincent de Paul second hand store. Intermingled between businesses were several residences whose owners had refused to sell to commercial interests.

The *hierberia* added a cultural dimension. As children, we did not understand fully but we knew people went there for all kinds of remedies. One could buy candles to burn for special intentions and not always rooted in good. One could find herbs to burn like incense, others to ingest as a tea for all maladies of body and spirit. The *hierberia* offered statues and prayers to address all situations for family, for relationships, to ward off evil spirits, and bring good fortune. It was a blend of genuine religious intention, folk medicine, and superstition. Many of the herbs are still used today for physical ailments. However, the sisters at the Catholic school never sent us there to buy candles or to take our prayer petitions.

Shoe shine boys were common, roaming the street with their wooden boxes strapped over their shoulders. They were hustlers for the small change paid to them. For children, small change was big money especially on a good day of business. As a child, I admired their hustling spirit at such an early age. I never asked for a shine since, as a child, I always wore tennis shoes.

The Mexican downtown had its entertainment district as well. The *cantina* section was around the corner. Many bars lined the street. All these bars looked a little shady, but that was my perspective as a child. I knew they were not the tourist destinations advertised by the Chamber of Commerce.

These cantinas were familiar to us as children. Our basketball coach at Catholic school would sometimes be absent from practice after school, and we would find him enjoying a brew. From the door, we could spot him, sitting on his barstool —presumably not reviewing play strategies for the team. Our better sense told us not to drag him out to basketball practice in his condition. We never won a championship. That was one bar he never reached.

Coming back after college, I entered one of those shady cantinas for the experience. I immediately was challenged by an  11-year-old boy who was playing billiards. My college diploma did not prepare me for this as I was beaten brutally in three straight games by this young hustler. "Welcome to the real world," I thought, "too much head knowledge and not enough life experience."

I excused myself at the fourth challenge. The loser always paid for the next game; and I clearly fit that category. I informed the bar room urchin I had an appointment. I preferred lying than facing another embarrassment. The hustler retreated to his corner, waiting for the next sucker to be lured in by his deceptive innocence.

Every city has its history, a unique cultural development. I did not see this as a child. It was just part of growing up. This was our town, our experiences. The new generation has moved in and has replaced much with modern venues. The *cantinas* were renovated and now disguise themselves as reputable lounges, restaurants, and bar-and-grill establishments. New memories will be formed by the current generation; and the old memories of the original buildings with the the cultural richness of the neighborhood will fade into history.

I often wonder if the bar room urchin remained in the district. Perhaps today he is owner of one of the entertainment establishments. I remain too embarrassed to check this out.

CHAPTER 46

The Beetle

I MUST HAVE BEEN swimming in the pool of boredom that day—nothing to keep me afloat, sinking fast into mindless existence. It was Saturday, and I had looked forward to doing something fun. With no school, every kid looked forward to the weekend.

However no friends could be found that morning; and that meant no neighborhood football game, no cycling about town, no hanging out of any type, no one to share in my boredom.

Sitting in the backyard, a large beetle crossed in front of me. I chuckled at its shape—a small head with two whiskers protruding, and a large rounded body being dragged along. I was grateful we humans did not have such a shape; and I began to imagine how different our lives would be if we had those proportions. Our heads would be the size of a football and our torso the size of a car. The images entertained me as I imagined myself with this shape going through a typical day at home and school.

I was intrigued as the beetle made its way through the yard. It moved fast, either being late for an event or with an important agenda for the day. The bug showed intent, and I was determined to find out what it was. I followed the beetle as it trampled over leaves and under small branches which blanketed the ground.

The beetle showed no discernment in its path—powering straight ahead—no going around or seeking an easier route.

If he had a wife waiting for him, I anticipated trouble. He charged with an attitude.

The beetle continued with increased speed and resolute determination, stomping over a regiment of ants foraging food for their community. Agitated by the rude intrusion, the ants blurted out a collective grumble, picked up their loads, and  returned to their chores. The beetle ignored them—no courtesies, no apology, not even an acknowledgement of their presence.

The beetle came to an abrupt stop as he slipped his head under a leaf. Did he think he was hiding? Was this his destination? Was this a rest stop? Was he meeting someone here? Ten minutes and no movement. I nudged him with a twig to prod him on his way. Not a flicker, not a twitch.

Watching a beetle under a leaf was no longer entertaining, and I returned to the house. By this time, friends were calling; and a football game was forming in the neighborhood. A light drizzle could not drench the spirits of kids on a Saturday afternoon.

I never saw the beetle again. He was gone when I checked later in the afternoon. I often wondered what became of him. No one really cared; none of my friends expressed any interest. He was just an insignificant beetle who crossed my path that day; but without effort or awareness, he pulled me out of my boredom. That was significant, and for that I was grateful.

CHAPTER 47

Dark Memories

THE NIGHT WAS unusually dark—not unusual for the area but unusual for a city dweller. I had forgotten the number of stars that shown in the isolated corners of nature. I had become accustomed to the city. Bright was my normal. There were few stars in the city.

Big Bend National Park in west Texas awakened me to the bigger reality. I sat in my makeshift seat—an old log which had shown wear and had obviously been used by other campers who had taken time to gaze into the heavens. The small clearing on the cliff's edge provided the perfect vantage point to stand in wonderment of nature's showpiece. The stars blanketed overhead like an expansive umbrella.

"Where did all these stars come from?" I wondered as I sat in awe. Decades had passed since I had seen so many. My tongue was in paralysis; words could not capture the magnificence of the sight. I could only sit in silence, enraptured by the blanket of stars that hovered over me. Two hours passed, broken only by the call by others to return to camp.

When I left Big Bend, I departed with an image sealed in my memory. The beauty of the night sky had captivated my attention, but I knew I would return to my world of perpetual brightness. I feared that I would forget my experience. As predicted, within a week, I was consumed by my old routine at work. It is easy to fall into our patterns, the usual, the typical everyday lives we live.

At times, I fall back to my camping experience at Big Bend. The opening of the sky at night opened my soul to the reality that life is bigger than the limited life I had created for myself. The stars were not new, placed there for tourists and occasional campers to appreciate. They have been there all along. I am the one who had failed to see them.

Seeing the sky during the day was only half the experience; the night exposed the other half, the fuller reality. Right now, I live in my bubble, seemingly content and foolishly thinking I am living to the fullest. Some day, I will venture into the dark and discover the fuller adventure of life.

I often wonder what the fullness of being me would look like. I question whether I am holding back because of fears or ignorance. Much of my life is still living in the daylight. I should not fear the dark. Life awaits to be discovered, to be developed. Life is like that.

"Children deserve an experience of nature, a retreat from the busyness of life. Nature provides the balance one's spirit cries out for—the stillness, the silence, the calming of soul. Every child should learn early."

CHAPTER 48

Portals to the Past

THE FLUFF OF COTTON candy, expansive as it may appear, can be squeezed to golf ball size in one hand. Life is like that. Decades of living through childhood and adolescence are pruned and reduced to morsels of memories. These morsels are often hidden from consciousness. They lie within, swimming in the pool of days gone by. Many sink to the bottom, lost and forgotten, never to surface again.

As an adult, I wade into my pool of memories. Initially, the entry is dark and murky with no clear images. However, my senses serve as portals of discovery. With eyes closed, I relax and allow my mind to float freely, to be led by the emotions of the senses. Like a fine mist rising and shifting, images of childhood begin to emerge.

"Ahh, the aroma of *tortillas de harina* on the *comal!*" As a child, I waited for the flour tortillas on the grill. I enjoyed patting the tortilla, popping the pockets and releasing the steam until it reached perfection in texture and color. The smells remained fresh, the memory just as fresh.

Corn tortillas were different. It was the sense of taste that triggered memories. A hot tortilla off the grill was always good by itself, but a sprinkle of salt onto a rolled tortilla created a perfect blend of ingredients. The taste buds always reacted with gluttony; my eyes responded in search for another tortilla.

"I could sneak one past my mother," I thought. Her line was always the same, "Wait for dinner or we won't have enough tortillas for the family." I usually managed a second. We always had enough tortillas.

Smell and taste triggered the most memories, but *tripas* and *menudo* were foods in their own category. These two were about texture. Intestines and stomach did not sound very appealing to us as children, but the Spanish words softened the mental images and converted them to tasteful dishes.

All depended on who was preparing them and how they were being prepared. Undercooked or boiled *tripas* were soft and slimy, like swallowing a live worm wiggling down the throat. Undercooked menudo was spongy, like swishing Jello in your mouth.

Sesos or cow brains never made my food list, but they were popular in Mexican culture. When given a choice between s*esos* or *tripas,* it was a no-brainer. I would choose the intestines any day, even if undercooked.

As I grow older, memories fade into isolated incidents of childhood. Specific ages—was I five or six—dissolve into "when I was little." We forget most experiences. Our senses, however, serve as portals to the past. Sometimes, the triggers relive positive experiences, and we relish those moments. Other times, they take us to episodes of sadness, grief, and unwelcome thoughts. The portals to the past expose what shaped us as children. We can embrace the positive and find peace from those moments. We can also embrace the negative and entertain them as opportunities for healing our wounds of childhood.

CHAPTER 49

The Question of God

STUDENTS IN CATHOLIC school expected to hear about God. Sisters lived up to their calling and ensured God was part of our curriculum in religion class, in prayer, and in going to Mass. However, this was not the first time we had heard about Him. In our early years as children, we were introduced to the idea of God within the family. I do not recall how old I was when God was introduced to me. I know it was not a formal introduction—no names, no handshakes, no "Glad to meet you" or other niceties exchanged. It was a gradual and smooth introduction which we accepted.

At school, we were taught God made everything, he knew everything, and he was everywhere. Words like omnipotent, omniscient, and omnipresent added to God's grandeur and mystery. For very young children, that was dramatic and incredible; but as children we believed, accepted, and showed no surprise. We prayed, went to church, and learned about Him. We did not question God's existence.

After 8th grade, all students moved on from the Catholic school. Adolescence opened the mind to other ideas. God lost his credibility. Friends dispersed in many directions—some leaving their roots to other denominations, some remaining faithful to the Catholic tradition, and others who lapsed into dormancy as inactive Catholics. God knows if anyone became an atheist.

The existence of God remains one of life's biggest questions. At some time, everyone faces this question. Some accept; some deny. Some argue to the grave in favor or against. However, if God exists, His reality goes beyond anyone's profession, anybody's reasoning, anyone's beliefs, or anyone's opinion. He is or He isn't. We have no say about it.

This is part of life's journey which demands a response. No one escapes it. Even lack of acknowledgement is a response. For me, I will continue to believe in the existence of God—unless He tells me otherwise.

CHAPTER 50

The Big Bang

THE 4TH OF JULY always marked our summer break—still two months before we returned to school. It was also Independence Day which meant festivity and celebration. The city kicked off its annual parade. Floats with traditional red, white, and blue caravanned down Main Street. High school bands resounded with patriotic tunes while onlookers clapped with approval and joined in their enthusiasm. Spectators cheered as fire trucks approached—lights flashing, sirens blaring, and firefighters in full regalia. A swell of appreciation resounded from the crowd.

Army vehicles were the highlight for the children. We had a fascination with jeeps, transport trucks, cannons, and especially the tanks as they rumbled down the street with an eerie sound of approaching danger.

Mounted horsemen, members of the local sheriff's department, marched gallantly—the horses in staggering compliance shouldering the weight of the paunchy patrol. Closely behind were the pooper-scoopers, a crew of eager youngsters who would otherwise be anonymous spectators on the curb, now finding their moments of fame carrying long-handled pans scooping up freshly emitted droppings. It was a dirty job but worth the explosion of cheers from the admiring crowd, rousing greater accolades than the politicians who followed.

The clowns—always receiving an explosive welcome in the parade—zigzagged through the streets, circling on their unicycles between floats and teasing the small children who sat on the edges in wonderment. Dubious about the outlandishly-clad characters with painted faces and fabricated smiles, a few children screamed in fear and clung to their mothers.

July is always hot in South Texas; and by mid-morning, even the air of celebration could not cool the searing heat of exasperated spectators. Exuberant cheering had diminished to polite waves and occasional singular claps in the crowd. The last entry in the parade passed unnoticed as families dispersed to shaded grounds.

As children, we knew the 4th of July was about independence from England. We had heard about Paul Revere and his famous ride, Patrick Henry and his ultimatum, and of course Benedict Arnold as a despicable turncoat. But the 4th of July was special because it was one of the few holidays when we could purchase fireworks. Children and fireworks provided the perfect combination for imagination and mischief.

Our stash of saved coins gave us access to the arsenal—bottle rockets, sparklers, flying saucers, and egg-laying chickens. These provided the entertainment, but the serious provisions were in the firecrackers. Any child experienced in explosives acquired a personal cache of Black Cats. They were the mother-load of all fireworks, produced for children on a mission.

Girls did not favor the firecrackers, unless they were the dainty Lady Fingers. They preferred colorful sprays and sparkles; boys sought booms and destruction. Loaded pockets of Black Cats provided ammunition for the afternoon. The patrol of neighborhood kids was ready, and the ant hills were always the first target. Weeks of work by the red ants were destroyed in minutes.

As kids, we blew up anything that would make a scene. Tin cans, rotting fruit, mounds of leaves all became vessels for explosives. The catapulting of the can into the air and the splat of rotten oranges were fascinating, but even these lost their excitement. Our imagination always sought novelty and a better blast than before. "What about our models," someone suggested, "We haven't tried those yet."

We were older now, and we had outgrown toys in our collection. We had grown up making plastic models of airplanes, cars, battleships, and popular monsters like Dracula, Frankenstein, the Mummy, and the Creature from the Black Lagoon. They lined our shelves; and at one time, they were our prized collections. Now they were prime targets for demolition.

The occasion was memorable. The battleship was long and made of durable plastic. All agreed a single firecracker would have no impact. Explosives were loaded at both ends of the ship in packs of three. They were ignited simultaneously, and everyone took cover to avoid anticipated shrapnel; but not all the firecrackers exploded at the same time.

Seeing one which had not exploded, I rushed, picked it up and held it high like a trophy and exclaimed with excitement, "Hey, this one is still lit." The boom rattled my ear; the blast pummeled my hand into a pulsating shock. My fingers were all intact; my ego was not. I endured the ridicule and tease of my peers, all done in jest and well-deserved.

I do not remember how old I was at the time of this incident, but I had to have been very young. Sometimes we do things we cannot explain except by blaming it on the ignorance of being a child. Sometimes, it is better to admit the idiocy of our actions.

CHAPTER 51

Slaughter

"YOU CLOBBERED MOM on the head." As children, we were not raised to be violent. However, there were times when we could hit our mother and even sock her in the head, stomach, or back. The most she would do was chase us and try to hit us as well.

Slaughter was a game of strategy, a game of war. Easter Sunday barbecue was the gathering for family; and while the men huddled around the pit poking at chicken and recycling old jokes, the brothers and cousins joined in this aggressive game. Our mother joined, not knowing what to expect. As mother, she garnished our respect; but in Slaughter, she lost her standing. She was an opponent, an enemy, a target to be attacked.

I do not know who developed the game of Slaughter, but the weapons and rules were home-made. We searched our drawers looking for old pairs of socks. We each had at least one pair with holes in the toes or heels or which no longer had elastic to hold them up. Everyone had a stash of socks which lost their match—a perplexity experienced by all, how single socks would mysteriously disappear. After keeping them for three months with the aspiration their pair would be found, the single socks were finally relegated to the game.

The socks were stuffed with newspaper, but there was a method to weapon production. The paper was rolled tight, soaked in water, squeezed to prevent over-saturation, and then sun-dried. This left them hard, firm, and malleable to the grip. Each of us had a preference, a custom design. Too much paper, it was too large to grasp. Not soaked enough, it would crumble easily.

At least thirty weapons were needed to arm the neighborhood for our war games. We divided into teams, challenging each other until the last man standing. The weapons were divided evenly, and the game would begin. It was not sufficient to be a good aim. It took maneuvering, attacking, retreating, and dodging. This was not a nerf ball for the weak or prissy character. This was Slaughter.

Our bodies took a beating. We were nicked, slammed, and clobbered by the hardened socks. We were scraped, scratched, and bruised from diving, sliding, and dodging the weapons thrown at us. We tripped over bushes, slipped on the wet grass, and fell into sticker patches. Nothing stopped the play  —too much adrenaline, too much fun—unless darkness set which was the indicator we had time for two more rounds.

Slaughter was an outlet which allowed us to fight with friends, get even with brothers, and even attack our mother when we played this game. No one was injured seriously, and no hard feelings were ever harbored. It was clean fun. It was a creative game. It attracted throngs of neighborhood kids who engaged in war games which sometimes lasted for hours.

Our mother's participation on Easter Sunday was a first for us as children. We saw a side of her that was foreign to her stature as a parent. She ran, jumped, dodged, and attacked as if she had previous combat experience. She played like a child and enjoyed the game, even though we clobbered her with no mercy. Easter Sunday was the first day she joined us in

Slaughter; Easter Sunday was the last day she played. She held no grudge, but extra chores during the week made us wonder.

The game remained in the neighborhood for several years. We went through many socks. Just as no one remembered how the game originated, no one knew when it faded away. I imagine we all grew up. Life changes for no apparent reasons. Life is like that.

CHAPTER 52

The Old Days

I WOULD NOT REPLACE today to return to the "good old days." Too much has changed for the better, but much also has been lost.

Growing up in a small community, life was simple then. We walked the streets, day or night, alone or in company. We rode our bikes freely around town and parked them downtown or at a grocery store without chaining the them to a pole. As expected, we found our bikes as we had left them.

We had sleepovers without fears, we played with friends in the neighborhood into the dark of night. We slept with our windows open to take advantage of nature's air conditioning. We left the front door unlocked when leaving for a few hours. We coordinated neighborhood games of football and baseball, rounding up whoever could gather at a moment's call. We were gone for hours without adult supervision, returning home in time to eat dinner.

Childhood was accompanied by our naive perception of life. However, we knew which neighborhoods to avoid and which kids were bullies. Parents knew generally where we were, confident we were involved with healthy and safe activities.

We gave them no reason to suspect we were involved with questionable behavior. Bad things did happen in the community, and we were not invincible; but our circle of friends and activities supported a high probability we would be okay.

Children today may find it difficult to imagine what it was like to live with such freedom. Today is their reality, and their filter for viewing life is blurred with constant broadcast of the the evils that occur in society—in the world, in the nation, in their local community.

There is reason for fear. There is reason for parental worry for their children being left alone or when too much space is allowed for them to get into trouble. Evil surrounds them.

Those who have never experienced what was lost—the freedom that was prevalent—do not know what they have missed. Those who have never had it may even find it difficult to imagine what could be.

We all conjure up memories of our past. For some, they were the "good old days." To me, they are just the old days. I do not wish to regress, nor do I venture to live in my fantasies of years gone by.

All I have is the present, something I have brought with me since my youth. I find that a great place to be, and I carry it with me everywhere I go. Now because of age, I can settle and savor my good old days.

CHAPTER 53

The Pizza

"SIT ANYWHERE YOU LIKE, and I will be right with you," the young lady addressed our group of eight as we entered the pizza joint. She handed us a menu and returned after a few minutes. "What would you like?" she asked politely with a forced but pleasant smile.

"I will have a medium pizza, half pepperoni and half sausage. One of my favorites," I said.

"Okay" she responded, "and which side would you like the pepperoni?"

I heard her response, but I let it filter through my mind wondering if I had understood her question. I chuckled internally but kept a serious face. "Hmmm. Make it the right."

After a brief hesitation and clearing of throat, I interjected, "No, put the pepperoni on the left. I think it tastes better." The server began to show a little agitation with my indecisiveness.

Our group was a little rowdy which apparently irritated the server as she slammed our drinks on the table. We requested a different server because of her hostile attitude; and the manager quickly complied. Apologetically, he explained that the young server was on her first day on the job. She was nervous, stressed, and having a difficult time. With her luck, she was given our rowdy group as customers. I do not think she ever realized the idiocy of her question.

We did not offer an apology to her, although it would have been appropriate. I laughed to myself with her question, but I did not criticize her. I too have had my moments.

On one occasion, while trying to settle a scheduled payment, a confusing dialogue ensued. In my frustration, I blurted out, "Wait a minute, you are saying the 18th is Thursday; so if that's the case, what day is Wednesday?" Sometimes I think the mind does not synchronize with the mouth, and we come out with idiocies.

On another occasion, a young man informed me of his brother who had passed away. Trying to show empathy, I responded, "I'm sorry to hear that. How did he pass?"

He responded, "I don't know. One day, he just woke up dead." I found it difficult, but I kept a straight face and followed up with compassionate remarks. Laughter or even a hint of a smile would have shattered the relationship I had with this young man.

Putting our foot in our mouth is a universal experience—the difference being that some do it more often than others. I am in that pool of having these experiences; and I do not mind as long as it is my foot and my mouth. I have learned to laugh at myself, still catching absurdities that flow from my mouth.

I am waiting for my next experience, knowing it is a matter of time. It is inescapable. Life is like that.

CHAPTER 54

Five Feet From Death

THE TIRE ROLLED DOWN the highway, a bit unusual. It was alone and gaining speed as it bounced down the road as if it had a plan. Worse, it was heading in my direction which prompted me to pull onto the shoulder.

A large utility truck was ahead of me, and the tire freed itself from the bed and bounced onto the highway giving it the momentum to terrorize the road. Vehicles ahead of me managed to avoid the potential catastrophe, and the tire slowed and found rest in the median. Still on the shoulder, I gasped a sigh of relief that the situation had resolved itself without consequence. My thoughts were premature.

"Bam," a loud crashing impact jolted my car. I ducked onto the front seat as images of a drive-by shooting flooded my imagination. The sound of a boom and a crash. No one had hit my car from behind, but it had shaken violently. Shocked, a bit nervous, and still unsure of what had happened, I peered into the rearview mirror to see the back window totally shattered supporting my suspicion of a shotgun blast. Was this a random shooting by some crazed individual who was expressing his rage on the highway, or was I being targeted?

I exited the vehicle slowly to inspect the damage. A large dent was on the side panel. Something had smashed it but it was not the damage from a shotgun. I searched the grounds around the vehicle and the evidence appeared. A metal cylinder on the highway had been projected by a passing vehicle, their tire hitting at a perfect angle to propel it at great velocity into my car. The investigation revealed the metal had also been dropped from the utility truck, the piece that should have been bracing the tire.

That morning was like any other day. My schedule was routine; my travel routes were ordinary. As if in slow motion, I witnessed a scene unfolding which broke the usual patterns of life. In the end, I found myself five feet from death. If the pro-

jectile had hit the driver's window, my head would have been the target; and it offered no defense against the force of the object. I would be dead, or perhaps worse, put into a vegetative state for the remainder of life.

"Five feet from death," I thought. "If I had parked on the shoulder just a few feet back, I would have been on the direct path of the projectile and likely would have been killed."

Incidents like this cause moments for reflection—a time of gratitude and appreciation for what we have and relief knowing what could have been. They help us to refocus on the important elements of life. I was ecstatic to be alive. Within those five feet, death was very close; but in perspective, death is always a moment away. We have no control over some things. We have witnessed those moments with people we know. Time is given to all, but we will all have our moment reserved particularly for us. Life is like that.

CHAPTER 55

Halloween

WORD SPREAD QUICKLY. Popcorn balls at the corner house. Halloween was a favorite holiday for the kids in the neighborhood. We waited for sundown and hit the streets with our grocery bags, hoping to fill them with candies and other sweets from neighbors and strangers alike. We ventured beyond our immediate neighborhood to any house with a light on. "Trick or treat," we all yelled in unison.

We were not a family that bought costumes. We did not want to look like everyone else in the neighborhood nor did we want to buy an outfit to be used only one day. The sisters at school would not allow me during the year to come as a peg legged pirate with an eye patch or as an Indian with a painted war face and a tomahawk. These were stereotyped images but as kids, we did not have the cultural awareness nor political sensitivities of today. In any case, we sought out the scary characters; horror movies were popular and scary masks were in.

My favorite was the Frankenstein mask with a ghoulish face, blackened eyes, and the classic scar across the forehead. One had to take on the persona, walking stiff-legged with arms outstretched and staggering down the sidewalk.

Some years, we designed our own costumes, looking through closets for ideas on what to wear. As last resort, we converted old sheets, poking holes in them and spooking the neighborhood as ghosts. As children we played the part. We were ghosts, flapping and sweeping through the streets as spirits taunting others. We were spooky and authentic—through our eyes as children.

Each year, the Catholic school held its Halloween festival. Children dressed in outfits without any restrictions—devils, angels, hobos, magicians, genies, zombies, and monsters of all varieties. Blood and scars were prevalent among the boys. These were entertaining, but they could not compete in the costume contest. One little girl, conniving at her young age, cloned herself as a miniature nun. Her outfit was identical to the sisters of the school. There was no contest. The sisters always picked her; and no one could appeal the decision. We allowed the nuns to bask in their bias while the rest of us headed to the food and games.

In the spirit of the school festival, we designed a spook house in our garage at home. It was an old wood-framed structure with rafters, complete with roaches and spiders as year round inhabitants. Neighborhood kids bought tickets to make their way through the maze-like corridors and experience the fright of their lives. Our version of the spook house made the school's look like Disneyland.

Flashing lights, ghosts sweeping across the ceiling, hands creeping onto the shoulders of the kids, and monster figures popping out suddenly in front of them, all created a festival of fear. As children, the experience was genuinely frightening. The younger ones who did not want to be left out, chose to enter but ran out screaming.

The trick-or-treating was the highlight of the evening. Our goal was to fill our bags so our booty would last for weeks. We roamed the neighborhood—one candy, two candies, and sometimes a handful if the resident expressed delight in our costumes. We always received treats; and we never resorted to tricks, despite our threats.

Halloween changed over the years. Schools and churches began to offer safe havens for the children, providing supervised celebrations. Neighborhood trick-or-treating was discouraged. A few incidents had been reported in the news of razor blades found in apples; and there was fear that candies might be tainted with drugs.

Some churches demonized Halloween as a satanic holiday. Schools only allowed cheerful costumes—princesses, cartoon figures, and storybook characters. Catholic schools encouraged the children to dress as angels or as their favorite saint. Monsters were retired. Political correctness had become firmly rooted in the community.

For children of today, this has been the norm. They never have known the free-roaming of the streets, the taste of home-made cookies, nor the excitement of receiving candied apples and popcorns balls.

We knew good and evil; and dressing up as a ghoulish monster or even as a devil did not drive us to satanic rituals or activities. We were vampires who played the part of biting our friends and sucking their blood. We died many times as others drove stakes through our hearts. We mimicked Dracula, Frankenstein, zombies, and other fiendish and ghastly characters.

Life's culture has changed. It has become sterile. Society's mindset was redesigned to protect our children and offer a safe zone for all. It is well-intentioned, and probably a necessity today. However, I cherished the freedom, the imagination, and the creativity we experienced in childhood.

Some of it may be regained some day. The sad part is that children do not know what they have missed and how different it was. Life changes. Life is like that.

Halloween was a time for fantasy and imagination, but not only for the kids in the neighborhood. Our pets looked forward to Halloween with great excitement."

CHAPTER 56

Allowed To Be a Child

LIFE OFFERS ADVANTAGES to children. We did not know better or different. We did not see life from an adult perspective. We were just children. We did not think of being poor or rich. Our home was small but adequate. We did not realize that with five boys in the house, two parents, and a grandfather, we were really cramped—especially with one bathroom to serve us all. We lived life as it was.

Even with a small bathroom, we had the advantage of being all boys. Three of us could huddle around the toilet, aiming from different directions. It worked most of the time. A little spray was inevitable, but everyone got his share equally. No one complained.

We lived a comfortable but not luxurious life. Our parents never revealed to us their struggles in life. I am sure there were times when they worried about meeting expenses. As children, we were shielded from those concerns. They allowed us to play our roles as children and not be burdened with the adult issues.

Allowing us to be children was one of the greatest gifts our parents gave us. We did our chores. We were expected to go to school and to do our homework. Parents did not have to prod us to complete our work. We had the nuns to face if we had not completed it, and this provided motivation.

Our free time was ours. We filled it with adventure and activity such as Boy Scouts, school sports, and random fun with friends. As young children, we could be seen flying through the streets on our bicycles as we donned towels around our necks pretending to be Superman. We never saved the earth from impending doom from a meteor, but only because the occasion never arose. Unlike Superman who doubled as Clark Kent, friends recognized our identity without the cape.

We had our Super Hero favorites; and as a neighborhood, we initiated the Cosmic Comic Club. Our collective dues bought the latest issues of Superman, Batman, and the Green Hornet. We shared the library among the Cosmic Club members, but none of us was smart enough to realize the value of the comics for future collectors. The issues we purchased for ten cents are now selling in the hundreds or thousands of dollars.

In a similar way, we amassed a collection of sports cards. We bought the packet of gum, and we stored our players in an old cigar box. As we became older, we figured we had outgrown them; and we used the cards on our bicycles, pinning them to the spokes with clothes pins to create a flickering sound as we sped down the neighborhood streets.

The value of those cards today would have created a comfortable retirement fund, but we were children. No card or comic book could replace the opportunity of just being a child. We were allowed to grow and develop with the mindset of a child—to think, to act out, to play, to be mischievous, and to be our age. This was an important era in life, the value of which I am only beginning to appreciate.

The value of the cards and comics still teases the mind occasionally. If only we knew then what we know now, a lesson repeated many times in life. I am sure this will not be the last opportunity to use this line. Life is like that.

CHAPTER 57

The Way We Are

SHE SHOWED NO anxiety or nervousness. She came to her appointment as directed and sat in the chair awaiting my arrival. As a young woman of 28 years, she had had no success in marriage or employment. Her life history was generally flat and unremarkable. Her demeanor followed suit—little animation, no attempt to initiate interaction, and empty eyes.

Beneath her facade, she appeared to be a pleasant young lady, certainly not abrasive. I eased in with casual conversation to engage her at the simplest levels.

"Those are sharp looking boots you're wearing. Were they made in one of our local boot factories?" She lifted her leg and crossed it over her knee. "Look here. I have a big hole," pointing to a two-inch tear in the sole.

"Well, I like the style, and your blouse matches perfectly." "Thank you," she responded genuinely. "The blouse belongs to my sister, and I will tell her that you like it."

We shifted conversation to the purpose of her visit; but I was determined to break the facade of her personality. "As we were talking, I noticed the length of your hair—longer than most people's. How long did it take to grow it to your waist?" She quickly interrupted, "I didn't even wash it this morning."

I pushed no more to avoid the appearance of flirtation. I was hoping to find the hook that would lure her into acknowledging one positive trait about herself. It never happened.

Later in the day, I went to the mall for a change of environment, picked up a cup of coffee, and just sat on an isolated bench. I was pensive but I did not want to think. I sat, sipped my coffee, and just watched others walk by. I felt as if I were screening a movie with front row privileges. People streamed by in slow motion—some alone, others in groups, some serious, others loud, and others pacing with purpose as if on a time clock.

I watched and wondered how people become who they are. I had wondered how the young woman with whom I had spoken had become so damaged and become the person she was. After 45 minutes, I stood and joined the stream of life's actors passing by, and I noticed someone else had occupied the observer's bench.

Now I was being watched. His eyes steered toward mine, and I was sure he was wondering how I became the person that I was. Was I becoming a little paranoid? I had not come to the mall for psychoanalysis. It must have been the caffeine late in the day that was making my mind race with thoughts. I darted to another bench. I found more comfort in watching than being watched. My mind was still consumed in self-reflection.

Could I transform myself into another person if I were to make a conscious effort, or was I stuck in being my present self? Perhaps I had detoured in life and had become someone else instead of me. If I am not the real me, then who am I? Do I still exist or would I know if I returned to being me?

This was becoming too deep for me. My observations had crossed the line. I was being overly analytical, judgmental, self-scrutinizing, and cynical. All I wanted was a cup of coffee and some quiet time. I made my way for a refill. "DECAF, please."

CHAPTER 58

The Cockroach

COCKROACHES WERE night creatures—most of the time. With generations of experience, they have learned to cohabitate with humans with great ease. They came out of holes and crevices in search for food; and with five boys in the house snacking throughout the day, the roaches were guaranteed a buffet.

The American cockroach was a large species with a wing span that allowed them to flutter across the room—at times, finding rest on one's shoulder or head. This did not happen often nor was it our biggest fear.

We could swat them off our bodies onto the floor, chase them across the room, and lay a decisive stomp across their shell. At the right angle, this would create a sharp "pop," giving clear evidence we had killed them. We feared the night when we were asleep. The roaches were in control.

As children, we had heard they could crawl into the ear and find refuge in the brain. We had no hard evidence of this, but we had a few friends at school who seemed to be missing a few brain cells. We could only wonder and take care this would never happen to us. We hoped we had not already been invaded in the dark hours of night. Sometimes, we could feel that itch deep in the ear canal; and our imaginations went wild with images of a roach gnawing on our brain matter.

Oral tradition in the family described one of the brothers as a toddler crawling with whiskers coming out of his mouth. None of the five made claim being the one with the roach, but everyone agreed it was the other.

Everyone in South Texas had a cockroach story, if not at home, then at a restaurant. Everyone joked about finding a fly in the soup, but it was no joke finding a cockroach. On one 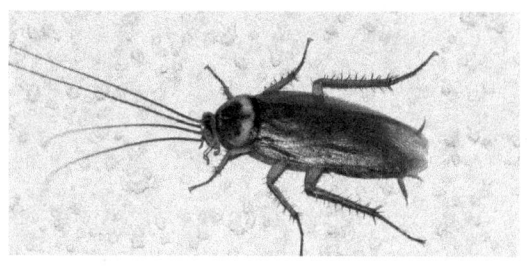 occasion at a local restaurant, a roach perked its head from under the table, emerged, and crossed the plate of enchiladas we were enjoying. After the initial disturbance, we managed to knock the roach onto the floor and squash it. We left the plate, disgusted from the experience.

We nibbled on food from the other plate, but we approached it cautiously. We knew roaches did not live in isolation, and we anticipated that another roach might emerge and attempt a food run across our other plate. We reasoned that if roaches were bold to sprint into the open, then how were they behind the scenes—at night in the food storage room, in the kitchen where the food was prepared, or on the dishes on which meals would be served? The images fed our imagination, but we could no longer feed ourselves. We lost our appetite, and we left after a few nibbles.

The restaurant offered a 50% discount on the one plate with the roach. While they acknowledged—without apology—that the roach may have been disturbing, they explained that the plate had been partially consumed before the roach made its presence. They wanted full price for the second plate because no roach had trampled on the food. We threatened to call the health department, and they welcomed it because they had just cleared inspection the week before.

Roaches have learned to share their environment with humans. Roaches have survived climate changes, catastrophes of nature, and human efforts to exterminate them. They have discovered the genetic code for perpetual existence.

As children, imagination and reality were indistinguishable. Did roaches really sneak through the ear canals at night? Did they find haven in the brain? As an adult, I have laid to rest those fears. I sleep at night without worry. However, given the history of roaches, I believe we are in for a lifelong relationship.

Rodrigo Codina, our father, 4th Infantry Division, U.S. Army, WWII

CHAPTER 59

Smoking

WHILE GROWING UP, we were surrounded by people who smoked. For many, smoking supported a habit; for others, it supported an image. In those days, it was legal for children to buy cigarettes. On many occasions, my father would stop at a convenience store, keep the engine running, and send me into the store to buy a pack of Winston. Only one question was asked by the cashier, "hard box or soft pack?"

Candy cigarettes were also common items on the shelves, and as children we indulged in pretend adult activity of smoking. We each developed a style or image of puffing and blowing smoke; but each shared a common goal of eating the candy.

Eventually, the candy cigarettes were pulled from the shelves as society judged them inappropriate for children. I am sure government studies determined candy cigarettes served as a gateway to vice. I had friends who as children had puffed on candy cigarettes and then as teenagers had been lured into marijuana. Perhaps a warning label on the candy cigarettes could have prevented this tragedy.

My grandfather also smoked. He preferred Camel, but he supplemented his supply with Bugler. This was for serious smokers who wished to roll their own.

He showed us grandchildren how to operate his roller apparatus. It was a four-step process but the last one was most challenging. We had to grasp the rolled paper, hold the tobacco tightly, slide our tongue along the gummy edge, and ensure we did not saturate the paper with our slobber. Our final product was often misshapen and bulky, but our grandfather never complained as we refilled his stash. In his latter years, he stopped smoking completely by going cold turkey; and we continued to use his roller as a toy.

Despite the frequent exposure to tobacco over the years, I was never attracted to smoking. Research on smoking showed it detrimental to health, contributing to cancer and lung disease. Commercials were graphic depicting individuals with emaciated bodies, gasping for air, and attached to life support. Statistics reported thousands dying each year.

Television commercials and magazines flooded the market to discourage smoking. Eventually, commercials promoting cigarettes were banned from television and radio. Despite efforts to raise awareness, smoking continued to be legal, popular, and widespread. Candy cigarettes were banned forever.

CHAPTER 60

The Violence We Bred

BY AGE 10 I ALREADY had owned five guns. The first was a pistol, dark green with a three-inch barrel. I selected it as my parents considered me responsible and ready.

I had friends—even younger than I—who already owned guns; and now I could join their ranks. This was memorable because now I could participate in Saturday afternoon water gun fights.

The model I chose proved to be inferior. It was a training model compared to the more sophisticated, high-powered pistols my brothers and friends had. My gun was soft rubber, one piece, with no trigger. I had to squeeze the body to squirt toward my target. I had little fun with it, but I knew I would gain the trust of parents to buy a better gun someday.

The plastic guns were durable with spring action triggers. They shot straight and had force to shoot at least eight feet with accuracy. When not shooting each other, we searched for mindless insects meandering in the field—roly-polies as we called them, earwigs, ants, and lizards whose scaly bodies hinted of prehistoric days. No creature was safe around the neighborhood kids.

The red ants were the insects of choice. They were always plentiful and busy, searching the ground for food or nest material. Some were seen dragging beetles ten times their size —pulling a few centimeters, dropping their catch, shifting their grasp, and taking it a little farther. The ants were persistent and focused until the neighborhood boys arrived with their water guns.

My first shot was a direct hit, separating the ant from its prey. Disturbed and dazed, the ant scampered frantically in search of his load. "Pow!" A second shot disoriented him and sent him into a mindless direction, empty-handed and bewildered. He abandoned his mission and scurried to the hole where he disappeared into his subterranean habitat.

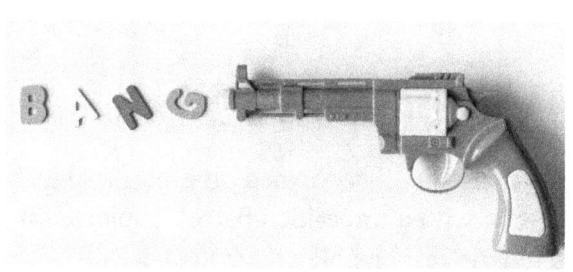

The red ants were not always out, but we had our method of stirring them up. We whistled into the hole. The ants surfaced, agitated and enraged; and they scanned the environment to identify who was disturbing the tranquility of their nest.

I do not know where the practice originated of whistling into the hole. I do not know why it worked. The whistling technique always existed, passed on through example and oral tradition; and anyone who played with red ants knew this technique.

During the sizzling days of summer when boredom set in, we challenged ourselves to see how many red ants we could collect. Finding an old pickle jar, we would go to one of the ant holes. Usually, there were at least two somewhere in the yard and one in the alley. The alley holes were larger and more populated because they were generally undisturbed by mischievous neighborhood kids.

My whistling was weak; but between the blows and squeaks, I managed to agitate the community. Out they came, fast and furious—first a few, then tens and hundreds. I grabbed them quickly and threw them one at a time into the jar. Speed was critical to avoid their mounting rage, but more importantly to avoid their pointed stinger, ready to contend with any intruder. Every child in the neighborhood at some time had been stung by these red ants, usually well-deserved for messing with their mounds. This time, I had avoided any bites or stings; and within thirty minutes, I had managed to collect several hundred ants.

With a screwdriver, I punctured holes on the metal top to allow air into the jar. I did not know the lung capacity of an ant, but I figured they needed oxygen.

I took pride in my capture, and I shared my harvested collection with family members. They were not impressed as they saw no purpose in my hunt. "What do you do with hostage ants?" they questioned. I had not thought that far ahead, so I just proudly displayed them on the kitchen table.

With no resolution, I decided to return the ants to their home. My plan did not go as anticipated. I dropped the jar, scattering shards of glass and confused ants in every direction onto the kitchen floor. In my panic, I stomped on all the ants. No survivors. It was an adventure gone awry; and this became my last hunt for ants.

The water gun fights dwindled among the brothers and neighborhood friends. Rather than retire our guns, we discovered we could fill them with Kool-Aid and take them on trips as makeshift canteens.

Eventually, we left the water guns and soon replaced them with cap guns which added the realistic "pop" when we shot each other. Dying correctly was challenging and dramatic. It was always a shot to the heart which was accompanied by the notorious grabbing the chest. Death was never instant, allowing us to demonstrate our theatrics and utter our dying words.

Each of us had a style, but it usually involved a roll onto the couch, a slumping to the floor, staggering a few steps, and ultimately a grimace of pain and finality. "Ugh, ugh.....ahhhhh!" The last breath was released. Our bodies succumbed to absolute stillness. Holding one's breath added to the drama as no movement could be detected. We died many times during those years.

We grew up in a gun culture. We played cops and robbers, cowboys and Indians, good guys and bad guys, and variations of war. We used guns, water bombs, and clod grenades. We shot each other in every imaginable way. Apart from the toys, kids grew up with BB rifles, knives, and shotguns.

It was common to see people with gun racks mounted in their trucks and pickups. Children carried pocket knives with them, even to school. No one saw them as weapons. They were handy tools; but most of all, they were just part of the stuff boys carried, along with marbles and loose change. I do not remember any of the girls carrying knives, even those who acted like tomboys.

Westerns, police shows, and war movies were common. Today, society blames the culture of violence on the exposure to media which today is much more graphic.

However, I do not believe that exposure to media is the root of violence. It is the lack of empathy and compassion which alienates people. The result is a society which is disconnected.

We owe it to our children to teach, to model, and to nurture empathy and compassion. These simple qualities build relationships, and they bond our connections with others. Violence finds it difficult to co-exist in this environment.

CHAPTER 61

Marbles

TODAY'S CHILDREN do not remember marbles, and they are clueless as to what to do with them. Marbles are a primitive form of entertainment compared to electronic and digital gadgetry of today; but in the old days, they were considered essential gear for any young boy.

There were many games we played with marbles, the most popular ones being Rings and Chase. Each game had different requirements but the key was being a good shooter. On a good day, I could win 15 marbles from opponents; but not everyday was a good one. Like the shootouts of the Old West, there was always one in town who was better and sharper at the hand.

Chase was not a creative game. The name says it all—one-on-one, taking turns, going after the other, and aiming to hit the opponent's marble first. Some players used a run-strategy, shooting their marble 15 yards with the expectations of a chase. These games would last 30 minutes with the only satisfaction in winning the opponent's marble.

The serious marble players were always ready. Packing marbles was part of the morning routine, a few in each pocket. On the right were my favorites, usually my select shooter marble with a good backup and a few others just in case. On the left was the collection of common marbles, those which were ugly or chipped—the marbles one would not mind losing.

Challenging another player was common at school. All the boys had their pockets packed and ready for the challenge. I do not remember any girls getting in the game or even showing interest. Gender dominant games were more clearly defined back then. Marbles was a boy's game. Girls were more into Jacks and Hopscotch. Not that girls were explicitly excluded from marbles, but I think they figured out that chasing someone else's marble for 30 minutes was a futile activity.

One particular day, I ventured into the playground ahead of the other students. I rested on the monkey bars and flipped upside down, hanging by my knees. Gravity set in, and all my marbles scattered on the ground. I panicked as my classmates were approaching with a look that they would loot my marbles. "Finder's keepers," I heard one yell with excitement as he began to run toward me.

"No way," I thought as I eyed my favorite shooter three feet away. In desperation and still hanging upside down, I let go at the knees forgetting there was space between my head and the ground below. My crown made contact, the ground providing no cushion as it had been hardened by the daily pounding of children's feet. I was dazed; and I scampered to recover what I could.

At some point, marbles faded with the times, or we matured as students. Maybe we just caught up with the girls and realized chasing marbles was a bit insane. Nevertheless, going through the marble stage was important. The games were simple, entertaining, and a learning experience.

We learned how to win and how to lose. We learned how to interact with others, to negotiate terms, to be flexible with life, and to be creative. We discovered we were responsible for our own entertainment and that boredom was a sign of a stagnant mind. Of course, in those days, we did not recognize our wisdom and that we were learning all those lessons for later in life. As a child, I just remembered it as the day I lost my marbles.

CHAPTER 62

Christmas Memories

I DO NOT REMEMBER when I stopped believing in Santa Claus. It was somewhere between 8 years old and when I was a junior in high school. I do not know how I discovered Santa Claus was not real. My parents did not break the news to me; my brothers did not tell me.

The sisters at Catholic school never promoted Santa but they never banned or degraded him. They emphasized the focus of Christmas being on Jesus and not how many gifts we received. I saw no conflict in believing in both Jesus and Santa Claus.

No specific Christmas story remains intact, but pieces of many Christmases fused together to form images and emotions. The anticipation of Christmas always stirred positive feelings—the fun of selecting a tree, decorating it with lights, choosing ornaments, and adding tinsel for that final sparkle.

One year it became fashionable to string popcorn and wrap it around the tree. The idea roused enthusiasm after we saw a picture in a magazine. The excitement fizzled quickly as it became a monumental chore. No one wanted to voice the problem. We were eating the stringed popcorn while we worked, and the project seemed endless. The following year, we stayed with the lights.

Christmas Eve put our family traditions into motion. Midnight Mass was always on the agenda. Every year, the old joke resurfaced, "What time is midnight Mass?" We never tired of the joke, and we always looked for a gullible friend to call the parish to inquire. I do not know which was funnier—when he made the call to the parish or when he reported to us that midnight Mass started at 12—all the time remaining clueless to the joke.

Midnight Mass offered a solemnity. As children, that meant it was going to be a long service. We learned to stay awake or to disguise our momentary dozing in prayerful poses. Hands folded, eyes closed, and a bowed head mirrored a meditative posture especially when kneeling. We rested our eyes until we had to stand up again.

The smell of bees wax from the candles, the scent of incense, joyous singing, bells ringing, and solemn prayers from the priest added to the special celebration. Further rejoicing followed when the priest in glorious voice and celebratory tone proclaimed, "Go, the Mass is ended," and we in joyful unison with the adults responded, "Thanks be to God."

Our parents never joined us at Midnight Mass. We were unaware this gave them the opportunity to do the Santa Claus magic by putting gifts under the tree. We arrived home by 2:00

a.m. The party began with the traditional eggnog, hot chocolate, buñuelos, fruit cake, cookies, hugs, Christmas greetings to all, and finally the excitement of opening gifts.

Eventually, nature took its course, and we all dragged ourselves to bed—sleepy, exhausted, but eager to wake in a few hours to play with our new toys and to see what others in the neighborhood had received.

At some point in my childhood years—no clear memory when it occurred—Christmas was no longer just about presents for us children. With my meager savings, I decided to buy a gift for my mother. I had no idea what to buy, and I eyed every item on the shelves of five-and-ten cent stores like Woolworths, McCrory's, and McClellans. They were within my budget.

After many hours and over several days, I locked my eyes on a small statuette of a Great Dane. I do not know how I finalized my decision on this other than affordability. We never had a Great Dane, and my mother had never expressed a desire for a statuette of a Great Dane. Nevertheless, I bought it with the right intention of giving my mother a gift for Christmas. She received it with surprise and happiness—or at least the portrayal of these emotions—and the Great Dane remained on display for years at the house.

My general feelings about all Christmases were positive. There were many thrills and a few disappointments in gifts we received. We had no idea of the struggles our parents went through to buy  presents for five boys. It was always safe to give us clothes, but our parents managed to provide some toys to all of us—a holster and gun set, roller skates, bow-and-arrow, or a board game. They knew the board games would keep us occupied for hours and away from mischief.

The oldest brother—being more mature and serious—received a chemistry set one Christmas. This fit his personality and studious nature. Years later and without surprise, he went to college and majored in chemistry. As a child, I was content with hula-hoops, poo-poo cushions, and blowing bubbles. These fit my personality; and while I believe they did not influence my college major, I carried this fun-loving spirit into my college years and into adult life. My parents knew us too well.

Culture and times change the experience of Christmas. Not all changes are bad; not all changes are good. As families and individuals, we set the tone for the celebration—for some a holiday, for others a holy day, and for a segment of society just another day. Some faiths do not hold Christmas within their traditions of belief.

Both religious and secular views of Christmas offer messages of tolerance and acceptance—providing a basis for peace and understanding, two critical components needed in today's environment. Unfortunately, not everyone adheres to these values.

The message of "peace on earth" is a universal call. It provides hope that life can be better, and each of us can do a small part to contribute to this ideal. Unfortunately, we continue in a world that shows little to no progress. Pockets of hope are still aflame, and Christmas reminds us of that hope. Life is like that.

CHAPTER 63

The Meeting Place

THE BASEBALL FIELDS were only five blocks away, an easy walking distance from the house. As children, anything within a mile was easy, especially on our bikes. Most kids in the neighborhood had bicycles, and we converged at the baseball park for many of our activities.

Some days, we gathered friends for a baseball game. We all brought what gear we had. We were always short on gloves but we shared, even if it meant using a catcher's mitt in the outfield.

Other days, we split into teams for kickball. This was more convenient when we did not have all the baseball equipment. For me, it was easier. It made more sense trying to kick a ball the size of a watermelon than swinging a long stick at a small baseball whizzing by at 500 miles per hour.

Football was our favorite sport and the one which attracted more of our friends. Surprisingly, no one was ever injured seriously—even when we played tackle.

During baseball season, the fields were actually used for baseball. The three fields hosted the Pee-Wee league, the Farm League for middle-aged players, and the Little League for the more advanced older children.

We attended the games frequently, not out of support for the teams nor the great interest we had in the sport. The park hosted a concession stand, and they rewarded free *raspas* or snow cones for every foul or home run ball returned. All the neighborhood kids loved baseball season just to enjoy cool *raspas* on a sultry evening.

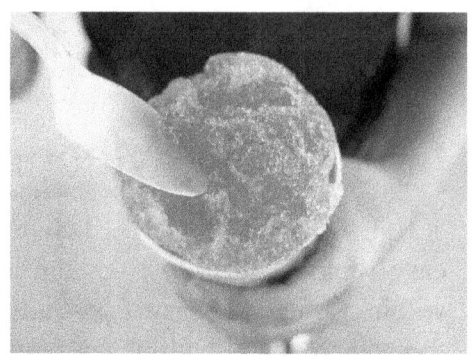

It was at the baseball park that I received a memorable injury to the head. Horsing around with other kids, I fell and hit the back of my skull on the bumper of a parked car. Vehicles were made like tanks, with steel frames and chrome bumpers. I left no dent on the bumper, but my head sustained an open wound. No one offered mercy or stopped the play; and I walked home with a bloodied head.

The baseball park served as a meeting station for events—in sports, in play, for all types of neighborhood activities. Eventually, the owners of the park converted the entire complex into a mobile home park without consulting with the neighborhood kids. Our playground was displaced, but little regret was expressed as most of the regulars had grown up and moved on to adult life.

We did not have the social media we have today. People depended on land lines and word-of-mouth. Some families did not have phones; and it required a race on bicycle to someone's house to spread the word of the impromptu football games. We would play for hours, pushing our fun to the edge of night.

As kids, we were active. We walked much, rode our bicycles even more. We gave it little thought at the time, but obesity was rare. We had our share of junk food—soft drinks, chips, cookies, and everything on the forbidden list of the dieters of today. We drank whole milk and chocolate milk, ate ice cream and donuts. We ate what we were served both at school and at home. Somehow, we survived childhood eating practices and transitioned into our adult habits. We like to think we grew up healthy; but perhaps our adult conditions are the results of all these choices.

As a child, the pyramid of foods was not relevant. We ate what was put on the table. No one was balancing the proteins and the carbohydrates. No one emphasized eating foods according to color or having specified servings of fruits and vegetables. We ate what was edible, regardless of shape, color, vitamins, proteins, or empty calories.

Today, all types of diets are recommended—for body types, blood types, to gain weight, to lose weight, to maintain weight, and sometimes to participate in the latest fad diet that promises the attainment of the ideal self. We are assured with all the credible advice on the internet which foods one must eat, foods one must avoid, exercises for maximum benefit, avoidance of activities that are detrimental, instructions on how to breathe efficiently, how to sleep properly, and even how to empty our bowels with efficiency. Life became too complicated.

There is much to learn. Ultimately, our goal will be achieved and we can be assured we will die healthy. As children, we did not know all these things; and we did what came naturally to us. We played a lot, staying physically active as time allowed. Our meeting place at the field was not just a place to play. It was the neighborhood health center.

CHAPTER 64

The Evil Within Us

"MORE COFFEE PLEASE" I signaled the server with a polite gesture. This was a request I regretted soon afterwards. I was sitting at the counter when a customer walked in and found a seat next to me. He immediately initiated a conversation with a question. There was no one else around, and the server rushed to the kitchen. Apparently the server recognized the man and made a move to avoid him.

The man did not introduce himself. He did not extend a customary "hello" or begin with a light-hearted comment about the weather.

"Do you know the mistake the Nazis made during the war?" he asked. I awaited in silence, expecting a punch line from an ill-humored joke. I gave a moment of thought and waited for his response.

"The mistake they made," the man answered, "was that they did not kill ALL the Jews." He did not wait for my reaction, and he continued to spew hateful comments. I did not respond as it was obvious he was not there for discussion or for my opinion. I tolerated his words for a few minutes and then found an opportunity to exit.

I did not see the man again. I felt no loss, but I wondered how much venom this man continued to spread. The hatred in this person was evil incarnate. He showed no reservation in expressing himself, even to a complete stranger. History speaks of many German officers who escaped after the war and fled to other parts of the world. I wondered if he had been one of them, secretly disguising his identity all these years.

I wish I had inquired more about him. Why did he harbor this animosity against the Jews? No person is born with hatred in his heart, especially to the degree he had expressed. What had he experienced in life to develop an attitude of loathing and repugnance for the Jews?

I have no answers, only speculation. Catholic school taught us the presence of good and evil in the world, a spiritual battle between God and Satan. The fallen angels were described as spirits roaming the earth with the mission of luring souls away from their Creator. This man put flesh on this imagery. I wondered when the tipping point in his life pushed him on the path of hatred. I am sure he is not alone; and the tug-of-war between the forces of good and evil continues.

He likely did not become this evil person at one given moment. Exposure to events and ideas over time and a series of life decisions led him to his current state. If this were the case, each of us is capable of falling onto the same path of evil by a slow erosion of our good spirit.

Unlikely? Perhaps he had said the same about himself. He may not have seen the incremental changes in the demise of his spirit. He may have seen his small decisions and choices in life as good. He may have been gullible to propaganda spewed by others, by his parents, by friends. He may have truly believed his perspective was correct and righteous. What stops me from going down the same path? Perhaps I am already on it, on a slow erosion of truth and good, blinded by denial.

CHAPTER 65

The Boy Scouts

BY STANDARDS OF accomplishment, I was not a good boy scout. I followed the example of my three older brothers in joining the organization; and that was the last of the example I followed. They rose through the ranks and earned bundles of merit badges. I passed the entry level of Tender Foot and earned a rank of Second Class—and the rest of my boy scout career remained there.

Despite my second class rank, my participation was not second class. I attended all meetings faithfully, engaged in scout activities, and attended Camporees and Jamborees annually. I joined others in five and ten mile hikes, participated in community volunteer programs, and carried my weight in troop activities.

It must have been a bad year in recruitment. Most of my peers who joined the scouts were of similar character. We had fun; we just did not aspire to higher ranks. On a camping trip, a friend and I sought to pass a requirement to become a 1st Class Scout. The task was simple, food preparation of any dish that would pass the inspection by our supervisor.

We kept the menu simple, a batch of home-made oatmeal cooked over the campfire. Two basic ingredients were needed, water and oatmeal. We did well with the water; the second ingredient gave us trouble. We presented our finished dish for the taste test to our supervisor who was also my brother. He took one taste, after managing to get a glob on his spoon, and announced the results. We failed.

The decision was disappointing, but after trying the oatmeal ourselves, we understood. A common belief for advancement says "It is who you know, not what you know." In this case, it made no difference.

After 8th grade and graduation from Catholic school, only a few classmates continued in Boy Scouts. When most of my peers and I did not continue, I heard no groans of disappointment from the scout leaders. Fifty years later, however, the troop still exists and remains strong.

We had our low-life performances and limited advancements in rank. Boy Scouts, however, was bigger than our failures. We learned that scouting was more than rank and merit badges. We benefited from the experiences, good and bad.

As an adult with family, I continued to enjoy camping and the outdoor experiences of "roughing it," a tradition my son has also carried into his adult life. Making a campfire, hiking the trails, and exploring the wild provide a balance to the niceties and comforts of city life. No greater satisfaction exists than to wake in the wilderness and to exit the tent to a brisk cold morning. No greater satisfaction exists than greeting the morning with a hot cup of coffee prepared over the campfire, poking at the coals to ease the chill, inhaling the fresh air in the woods—and sitting with a fresh bowl of oatmeal that would make any boy scout drool, a true first class experience.

CHAPTER 66

Preparing Our Story

BARRING EARLY TRAGEDY, everyone moves on to their adult years. There is no test to become an adult. It is not earned. There are no qualifications required, no proof needed except the birth certification that one has reached the age.

We keep moving along, running the treadmill of life until the motor gives out. I am still on the treadmill, and I wonder how much longer I have before the life-time warranty expires. It is a question we all face at some time. I will die someday; I am not exempt. It is grave matter, so to speak; but I am not depressed or morbid about it.

When I pass a cemetery, I see the hundreds of tombstones representing those who have already passed. Obviously, there are many who have more experience in dying than I do. The graves with their headstones, crosses, markings, and epitaphs

represent all—young, old, and many in between. The silence among the dead cracks, and the voices of our ancestors reach out to those who would be attentive. What would they share about life? What wisdom would they provide to us who are still alive?

I wish I could sit by each site and listen to the stories of these individuals who have died. Their perspectives about life would be unique, and their words would be filled with insight, credibility, and wisdom.

Stories are not meant to be buried and lost. They are for the living. They are for us who are still on the road of life.

CHAPTER 67

Reflection on Life

THE LANDSCAPE LOOKS different now. Looking back, I realized how much life has changed. People with whom I was close years ago have been filed into the archives of memory. These were people who were part of my daily living—friends in the neighborhood, classmates in school, peers in residence, and colleagues at work.

Growing up scatters everyone—different plans, going off to school, career choices, changes in direction, shifts in values. Hundreds fit this pattern, intersecting for moments in life—moments considered important, relationships deeply appreciated, friendships valued and seemingly indestructible at that time.

Some have died, a few passing at an unexpected early stage of life. They never reached the fullness of adulthood; and I wonder how they would be today if they had lived longer. Most are still alive—somewhere out there. Occasionally, a voice from the past surfaces, always a surprise. Sometimes we are able to reconnect with common feelings and memories, and old bonds are renewed. Other times, years or decades of living apart have eroded any feelings of connection and we move on as strangers to each other.

Life is in full flux. The only constant has been change. Even among family, change has been frequent. Most in the generation before me have vanished—grandparents, parents, uncles, aunts, cousins. The erosion has penetrated into my generation—the loss of siblings and peers—reminding me change crosses all boundaries. At times, a moment in life will trigger memories—faces from the past, people I miss, things we used to do, reminders of conversations, and just times of being together. I lost count how many people are gone now. The accumulative effect produces feelings of monumental loss and unresolved sentiments. The unresolved are moments of regret for not taking time to see someone or perhaps not coming to terms on issues that led to disagreements during life. With death, issues become insignificant and meaningless.

I am not alone. My experiences are common, shared by everyone. Imagine people in their 80's, 90's, and especially those who have arrived at the century mark. They have few if any peers remaining. They have had to find ways to cope through life, and they possess a treasure of information on how they have adjusted with so many losses. They have volumes of stories; and the rest of us owe them an attentive ear. It is not a courtesy to them; it is an opportunity for us to be enriched.

Life offers a crazy course of events—a blend of the expected and the unexpected. Life is never a straight line. Sometimes, life can be messy, unpleasant, and repulsive. Other times, life is smooth, refreshing, and fulfilling. Some individuals run the course better than others; and our stories give testimony to this. Adaptation to change is the key; and adaptation determines the outcome. Life is like that.

CHAPTER 68

Epilogue

THE STORIES YOU have just read are a sampling of my life. Most represented childhood years—selective, limited, and viewed from my perspective. My brothers' points of view would have given different twists to events. This is the nature of stories; and this is the nature of story-tellers.

Stories abound within every individual; and they lay dormant unless they are shared. A good story should not be wasted. The stories of old are the substance of what makes you who you are today. Digging up your past provides the opportunity to share these building blocks with family and friends. Through experiences, we gain insights and wisdom—even if measured with regrets, denials, and tempered through the hard knocks of life.

In today's environment, sharing is more of a challenge. Individuals are absorbed in their electronic devices and busyness of life. Self-entertainment frequently replaces communication and interaction with others.

The purpose of this book was to stir the life experiences within individuals. The stories that emerge—your stories—will provide entertainment, laughter, tears, morsels of wisdom with family and life companions.

Stories do not have to be dramatic life-changing events. Simple experiences gain meaning when they are filtered through your eyes and your interpretation. Sometimes, the simple events are the most moving, most impactful, and most treasured.

Connect the dots between stories and it forms a picture of life. Some people will point out that many of the dots of life were horrible experiences. Their life was filled with terrible events and toxic people, perpetuated by lingering memories. Their picture of life—after connecting the dots—resulted in being the miserable persons they are today.

But the dots are still being connected; and no person is destined to be miserable except by choice. Life continues to unfold, and it is not defined exclusively by the past. As we place more dots in the picture—experiences, events, people—we shape the stories we need for a happier, more satisfying life. We continue to lay the dots of our life. This is the beauty of the story; the story is the beauty of our life.

CHAPTER 69

Author's Final Words

My life has come full circle. Being born and raised in McAllen, Texas, I went off to school and returned ten years later. I chose to spend my career years in my community. I do not elaborate here on my work history out of fear it will sound like an obituary filled with a chronology of my life.

I have now entered my retirement phase. Retirement takes on different meanings to peers and friends. I know no one who lives the stereotype of sleeping late and lounging around all day. Most describe their lifestyle as "busier now than when I was working." This is consistent with my experience as I remain involved with church and community; and this has presented an unexpected and refreshing aspect. Retired people tend to bring themselves into a group—especially volunteer involvement— without their acclaimed status, earned titles, and professional reputations.

Individuals tend to accept each other as persons, much like we accepted our friends as children. There is no facade to maintain, no image to present, no need to prove one's abilities or to make claim to superior knowledge or experiences.

With retirement also comes a realization that we have more days behind than ahead of us. Questions about life take on new focus—how to live out the latter stage of life. This is not a morbid question but a practical consideration. I would like to finish my life in a meaningful way and not just wake up each morning waiting for my last breath.

I continue to be amazed how much I have changed over the years, how small incremental developments have brought me to my present form which is immensely different from my childhood picture above. I had no idea what lay ahead; and now as I look back, I can describe it as an interesting journey. It took me a lifetime to realize how short a lifespan is.

Not every family has a writer, but stories can be passed on by oral tradition but more effectively through audio or visual recordings. The story is the focus, and all families are rich with these experiences. The biggest challenge is making time while recognizing the value of having each other while we are still alive. Life offers us these moments but these too will pass. Life is like that.

www.ingramcontent.com/pod-product-compliance
Lightning Source LLC
Chambersburg PA
CBHW051943290426
44110CB00015B/2092